Socialist History Society

Telling the Mayflower Story
Thanksgiving or Land Grabbing, Massacres & Slavery?

Danny Reilly and Steve Cushion

Socialist History
Occasional Publication 43

SOCIALIST
HISTORY
SOCIETY

Published by
The Socialist History Society, 2018

ISBN 978-0-9930104-8-4

Front cover illustration: Pequot War from Libary of Congress

Contents

Replica ship Mayflower II at the State Pier in Plymouth, Massachusetts, US.

Introduction

It is a widely held belief that the history of the USA begins with the voyage of the Mayflower from Plymouth in 1620 carrying the Pilgrim Fathers to a new life on the North American continent. This sect of dissident Calvinist Puritan Protestants had set up a religious group outside the Church of England, and were fleeing persecution by the English King, who was also head of the Church of England. King James I had continued the practice of condemning the setting up of independent churches outside the state religious structure as illegal. Consequently, the *Separatists*, as this sect of Puritans were known, felt that they had to flee to where they could lead a new life, where they could live according to their consciences. This, it is often argued, laid the foundation of American freedom and democracy.

However, the official version leaves out more than it tells. The American continent was already home to many Indigenous Nations, numbering over 50 million, prior to Columbus's journeys in the late 15th century.[1] In the New England region where the Mayflower passenger colonists finally landed, only a few European fishermen, slavers and 'explorers' had been seen by 1620. The *Pilgrim Fathers*, who comprised half of the colonists on the Mayflower, were as intolerant of other peoples' religious beliefs as the Church of England was of theirs. Their belief in freedom and democracy only extended to members of their own church and they had no objection to selling the Indigenous population into slavery. Also, the Plymouth colony was not the first English settler colony in North America. This dubious honour goes to the slave colony of Jamestown, Virginia, which is not nearly such a worthy sounding candidate for a foundation myth. The full history is much more nuanced than the myth, and, if we are to understand the future development of European settlement in North America, we need a rounded account that includes the genocidal effects of this colonization on the Indigenous population, and New England's role in slavery and the slave trade.

The established *telling* of the Mayflower Story over the past 400 years has neglected the colonizing purpose of the journey and its aftermath on the one hand and has been restricted to the Separatist half of the Mayflower passengers on the other. This narrow, limited and ideological account of an episode in early English colonization of North America has been designed for political

---

1 Denevan, William M., 2012, *The Native Population of the Americas in 1492*, Madison: University of Wisconsin Press.

purposes. But we propose that the re-telling of this 400-year old historical episode should draw on the critical accounts of scholars of the Indigenous Nations of North America, the African American and African Caribbean communities, and others. The aim of drawing on such accounts is to provide context for the Mayflower Story by highlighting the background and consequences, immediate and longer term, of early English colonising of North America.

The Separatists had, prior to 1620, fled to Holland to escape religious persecution in England. They returned to England only temporarily to allow them to link up with another group of colonists, who were not of their religious persuasion, and who they labelled "Strangers". Together the Separatists and Strangers set off on a colonial venture similar to other such English journeys across the Atlantic that were taking place at that time. The Mayflower voyage was financed by a group of 70 London businessmen, the Merchant Adventurers, looking to make a profit once the colonists had taken land and established a settlement. By neglecting the wider colonial context and background of the venture, and the genocide and slavery that followed it, the historical account of the Mayflower's 1620 voyage and its significance is distorted.

The Mayflower passengers who started the New England colonies in 1620, are frequently taken as the Founding Fathers of the USA, hence their importance. But this English colonial territory was founded on land forcibly taken from the Indigenous Nations of the region. The effects of these early colonial invasions were devastating. There were approximately 500,000 people already living in the territory later occupied by the thirteen colonies at the beginning of the 17th century. Their numbers had dwindled to about 260,000 as a result of disease, warfare and dislocation by 1700.[2] In 1600, the territories of New Hampshire, Massachusetts, Rhode Island and Connecticut that were colonised in the 17th century had an estimated population of 60,000. By 1700 the region's Indigenous population is estimated to have suffered a 90% population decline. The land the English colonisers seized was used to establish a successful economy through trade, including the slave trade, with the English Caribbean slave colonies. Also, the methods used by the early colonists to clear New England of Native Americans established patterns of genocidal warfare for future "Indian Wars" in North America from 1700 - 1900. All this needs to be

---

2 Newell, Margaret Ellen, 2003, *Economy*, in Vickes, Daniel (ed), *A Companion to Colonial America*, Oxford: Blackwell, p.185.

told as part of the Mayflower Story because the previous commemorations that omit slavery, slave trading, land grabbing and genocide have created a shameful tradition of telling a sanitized account of early English colonialism and its aftermath.

The Mayflower Story itself has a distinct lineage of retelling linked to English and US colonial imperialist politics, and like other related commemorations, such as Columbus 1992, it has proved highly contentious. But such commemorations are not just historically controversial. The struggles of Indigenous, African American and Caribbean peoples over their rights has included, and continues to include, opposition to these sanitised accounts of history. Through this pamphlet we hope to help increase understanding and support in the UK, during the 400-year anniversary commemorations and beyond, for the ongoing struggles of the Indigenous Nations of North America, of African-Americans and of African-Caribbean peoples today.

Gov. Endicott landing on Block Island.

Artist: A.R. Waud (1876)

English Colonialism – where the Mayflower fits in
The Transatlantic trade
The Atlantic slave trade started in the late 15ᵗʰ century with Portuguese slaving in Africa and became a cross-Atlantic trade following Columbus's voyages from 1492 - 1504, sponsored by Spain. The Transatlantic trade, initially limited to Spain and Portugal, consisted of chattel slaves captured in Africa and traded for a variety of manufactured goods, including armaments. The African slaves were transported to the Caribbean, South and Central America, with some Indigenous American slaves being transported the other way to Spain and Portugal. Goods taken from the Americas to Europe consisted of gold and silver, as well as agricultural produce, such as sugar, grown on plantations by slave labour.

In the course of the 16ᵗʰ and early 17ᵗʰ centuries, the Dutch, French and English all sought to become part of this Transatlantic trade. Colonization and slavery were major issues in the European wars of the period involving these three countries along with Spain and Portugal. The problem for England in the 16th century was its relative economic weakness and so, like the Dutch, it initially resorted to piracy against the Spanish and Portuguese to get a foothold in the slave trade. To gain colonies, England targeted the Caribbean and the North American Atlantic seaboard, establishing its first continuous ongoing colony in Virginia in 1607.

The Virginia colony, operating as the Crown-licensed Virginia Company, had a major problem finding investors, colonial settlers and workers in England, which led the Virginia Company to sub-let 'patents' for colonial settlement ventures. One such was that undertaken by the Mayflower in 1620 which was backed by the Merchant Adventurers, a London business group.

European views on colonialism and slavery
Wars of invasion for the purpose of territorial expansion and enslavement were a feature of Southern, Western and Central European societies going back many centuries. However, the adherence in these areas to a medieval version of Christianity led to the formulation of a right to invade other lands that was bound up with papal power. Crusades against Muslim states were sanctioned and encouraged because these were considered a military threat, were non-Christian and included the areas designated as "The Holy Land". Other non-Christian nations were designated legitimate targets for invasion under the

"Doctrine of Discovery" initially detailed in papal bulls. Notable are those issued 1452/1455, permitting Portugal to seize land and slaves in West Africa, and the bull *Inter Cetera* of May 3, 1493 granted Spain the right to conquer the lands that Columbus had already found, as well as any lands which Spain might "discover" in the future.

The Treaty of Tordesillas of 1494 divided lands outside Europe between the Portuguese Empire and the Crown of Castile. A meridian was drawn 370 leagues west of the Cape Verde islands, off the west coast of Africa, about halfway between the Portuguese Cape Verde islands and the Caribbean islands of Cuba and the island of Hispaniola, modern day Haiti and the Dominican Republic. The lands to the west went to Castile because Hispaniola had already been claimed for Castile and León by Christopher Columbus on his first voyage. The lands to the east would belong to Portugal. The later Treaty of Zaragoza similarly defined the Spanish and Portuguese claims in Asia. These treaties did not consider any of the other European powers, which generally ignored the agreement.

The Treaty of Tordesillas declared that only non-Christian lands could be colonized under the "Doctrine of Discovery", which asserted that title to lands lay with the government whose subjects travelled to and occupied a territory whose inhabitants were not subjects of a European Christian monarch. Despite papal restrictions, the notion of 'discovery' was used to justify enslavement as well as war and territorial seizures. Also, undeterred by sectional differences, both Catholic and Protestant powers found the doctrine a convenient justification for the expropriation of Indigenous lands. A Massachusetts Bay Colony law of 1633 decreed that "*what lands any of the Indians have possessed and improved, by subduing the same they have a just right unto according to that in Genesis*".[3] Therefore, any land not so "*improved*" could not rightfully be held by the Native Americans but could be seized by the settlers.

Doctrine of Discovery still in use today

In 2010 a UN study established "*that the Doctrine of Discovery has been institutionalized in law and policy, on national and international levels, and lies at the root of the violations of indigenous peoples, human rights, both individual and collective. This has resulted in state claims to, and the mass appropriation of, the lands, territories, and resources of indigenous peoples.*

---

3 Thomas, G. E., 1975, "Puritans, Indians, and the Concept of Race", *The New England Quarterly*, 48, no. 1. p.11.

Both the Doctrine of Discovery and a holistic structure termed the Framework of Dominance have resulted in centuries of virtually unlimited resource extraction from the traditional territories of indigenous peoples. This, in turn, has resulted in the dispossession and impoverishment of indigenous peoples, and the host of problems that they face today on a daily basis." The study found not only that USA Supreme Court ruling *Johnson & Graham's Lessee* v. *M'Intosh* in 1823, had used the doctrine to the detriment of the Indigenous Nations of North America, but they also found evidence *"demonstrating that the Doctrine of Discovery continues to be treated as valid by the USA Government."* [4]

Indigenous Slavery

'Indian Slavery' in the Americas was started by the Spanish colonial power. However, it is important to remember that it continued in the North of the Americas as a result of its adoption by the early English colonists of Virginia and New England. This was then inherited as a labour practice by future settlement builders at different times in different territories across the North American sub-continent in the 18th and 19th centuries. In the 18th century *"Indian slaves were themselves a widely pursued and traded commodity, one that enriched early entrepreneurs from New England to Georgia".* [5] From 1492 to 1900 it is estimated that in the Americas there were in total, 2.5 to 5 million Indigenous slaves, of which 147,000 - 340,000 were enslaved in North America. [6]

The division and labelling of the Americas as two distinct North and South sections plus the Caribbean islands is relatively recent. Columbus's voyages in the late 15th and early 16th centuries led first to Spanish settlements and enslavement of Indigenous people in the Caribbean island of *Espanola* (or Hispaniola, modern-day Haiti and the Dominican Republic). These were quickly followed by invasion and slaving ventures to other Caribbean islands and the areas now known as Central America, South America, and the Southern fringe of the USA. From the early 1500s, European slavery in the Americas involved both enslavement of Indigenous people and the importation of Africans. The legal regulation of Indigenous slavery by the Spanish changed

---

4 Gonnella Frichner, Tonya, 2010, '*Impact on Indigenous Peoples of the International Legal construct known as the Doctrine of Discovery, which has served as the Foundation of the Violation of their Human Rights*', New York: UN Economic and Social Council, p.1.
5 Newell, 2003, *Economy*.
6 Resendez, Andres, 2016, *The Other Slavery*, Boston, Houghton, p.5 and Appendix 1.

over the course of the early 16th century. The 'New Laws' of 1542 sought to abolish 'Indian' slavery systematised in 1513 under the early '*encomienda*' system. However, in order to supply workers in the new silver mines a system of nominal wages for compulsory labour, known as '*repartimiento de indios*', was introduced. The Spanish colonists complied with "*the law in form but not in substance, and adapted Indian slavery to fit the new legal environment, and thus it became the 'other slavery*'".[7]

The *other* slavery

In the 17th and 18th centuries, under English and Spanish rule, as well as under later US and Mexican rule, enslavement practices in North and Central America followed this precedent of legal manipulation and renaming. The *other slavery* under different regulations or names, such as debt peonage, servant certification, debt transfer, child apprentices, compulsory work following charges of vagrancy and convict related forced labour, continued with variations in both time and territory into the 19th century, and in some areas into the 20th.[8] Though the 13th Amendment to the USA constitution, which outlawed slavery and 'involuntary servitude', was passed in 1865, the continuation of the peonage system, led to the *Peonage Abolition Act of* 1867 directed at this specific form of involuntary servitude practised against Indigenous Americans, particularly in the New Mexico territory. Yet the lack of enforcement of this law left many Indigenous people in a condition of what was still effectively slavery. Additionally, the *Civil Rights Act* (1866), the *14th Amendment* (1868) and the *15th Amendment* (1870) "*failed to bring relief to Native Americans held in bondage*". partly because they did not clarify citizenship and tax status of Indigenous Americans.[9] Eventually, legal clarification of citizenship was partly enacted with the *Indian Citizenship Act* (1924).

Slave society or society with slaves

Slavery, as an economic institution, developed unevenly, finding intellectual justification following the discovery of some commodities, such as silver, sugar or tobacco, which had an international market and the production of which required a larger labour force than was available locally. Ira Berlin distinguishes between a *society with slaves* and a *slave society*. In societies with

---

7 *ibid.*, p.75.
8 *ibid.*, p.238/9 & 306; Newell, Margaret Ellen, 2015, *Brethren by nature: New England Colonists and the origin of American Slavery*, New York: Cornell University Press, p.128 & 223
9 Resendez, 2016, *The Other Slavery*, p.305

slaves, slaves were marginal to the central productive processes and slavery was just one form of labour among many and the master-slave relationship did not set a social standard. When societies with slaves became slave societies: *"slavery stood at the centre of economic production, and the master-slave relationship provided the model for all social relations"*.[10] Slaveholding elites then also erected impenetrable barriers between slavery and freedom, and elaborated racial ideologies to bolster their dominant position.

Racism and colonialism

The original justification for enslavement and territorial incursion in the 'discovered' territories of the Americas and Africa, which was adopted in the 15th and 16th centuries, was that the inhabitants were not Christians. Europeans had for centuries justified war, persecution and discrimination against peoples of the neighbouring Islamic Nations and against Jewish people in Europe because their non-Christianity was deemed to apply to the whole population and to thus remove the need for Christians to obey such biblical injunctions as *'Thou shalt not kill'*. Drawing upon these earlier designations of whole peoples as fundamentally different, European thinkers developed the ideas we have come to know as racism. In relation to Africa and the Americas, an early crude racism identified the Indigenous peoples of the Americas as devil worshipping, uncivilized savages, and the peoples of sub-Saharan Africa as suitable only to be enslaved. Both groups were seen as lesser humans.

However, these crude justifications for genocide and enslavement were supplemented by new, more secular 16th century notions of 'natural law' and political freedom developed initially by Spanish intellectuals. This new economistic thinking broke with medieval theories of "just price" and included in their new theories of freedoms the concept of *commercial freedom*. The ancient Roman law concept of *'Jus gentium'* (the rights of peoples or law of nations) was used to explain why war to open free travel and trade, as part of colonization, was 'defence of the common' and 'self-defence' and was, therefore legitimate and just. Once a 'just war' has been declared, it can be fought to the end, *'and this is especially the case against the unbeliever, from whom it is useless to ever hope for a just peace on any terms. And the only remedy is to*

---

10 Berlin, Ira. 1998. *Many Thousands Gone: First Two Centuries of Slavery in North America*, Cambridge: Harvard University Press.

destroy all of them who can bear arms against us, provided they have already been in fault.[11] Needless to say, only Christian nations can declare a 'just war'.

Thus, the early colonialists had available to them a range of justifications, religious, secular and economic, to justify their colonization practices. Added to these were the legal designations of the land they seized as '*vacuum domicilium*' (unoccupied) or, '*res nullius*' (nobody's thing), and therefore considered ownerless property and free to be acquired by means of occupation. These ideas gave theoretical license to make war on the Indigenous peoples of the Americas and drive them off their land on the one hand, as well as make war on African peoples in order to enslave them on the other. Using the land cleared of its people, the European colonists were able to seize its resources of gold and silver, land and crops. King James I's 'New World' started with colonies in Virginia, New England and the Caribbean, where, initially, a new system of connected colonies based on indentured and slave labour, international trade and profit was established. The Mayflower journey started New England, the second prong of English colonisation.

"February 22, 1637" by Charles Stanley Reinhart, 1890

---

11 Francisco de Vitrias, 1532, 'Of Indians and the Laws of War" (*De Indis et de Ivre Beli Relectiones*) p.171, quoted in Bohrer, Ashley J. 2018. "Just wars of accumulation: the Salamanca School, race and colonial capitalism", *Race and Class*, vol. 59, no. 3, January - March. pp.20-37.

England's colonization in the Americas

The English colonization of the Americas had started in the late 15th century when Henry VII gave an English Crown licence to John Cabot's voyage to Newfoundland, which he claimed for the English King, but no settlement was established. Next, Elizabethan colonists, including veterans of the bloody wars of settlement in Ireland, were the first to try and establish what proved to be the short lived Roanoke colony in North America, naming it Virginia after the virgin queen, Elizabeth I. The Plymouth Company was founded in 1606 under James I of England with the purpose of establishing settlements on the coast of North America, but its colony in Maine was also a short lived failure. The small settlement established in 1607 at Jamestown in the modern State of Virginia is recognized as the first permanent English colony in the Americas. The colony was located on the land of the Paspahegh people, part of the Powhatan Confederacy. The Paspahegh initially welcomed and provided crucial provisions and support for the colonists. However, relations quickly deteriorated and the Paspahegh were exterminated within three years by war and disease. Mortality was also very high among the English settlers in Jamestown itself, with over 80 percent of the colonists dying in 1609-10 from disease and starvation.[12]

The failure to find enough volunteers to settle Jamestown eventually led to Virginia becoming a 'slave society', while the lack of success in finding financial backers for Jamestown led to the practice of selling leases or 'patents' for parts of the North American coastal region the English claimed.[13] One patent was for part of 'North Virginia', the area at the mouth of the Hudson River, but which was then the land of the Lunape people, and this was granted to the Merchant Adventurers for the Mayflower venture in 1620. As it transpired, the Mayflower ship never arrived at its intended destination but landed in the Cape Cod area on the Atlantic coast, and established a settlement called New Plymouth on the site of modern Plymouth, Massachusetts. This second colony started the creation of New England.

---

12 Charles M. Hudson & Carmen Chaves Tesser. 1994. *The Forgotten Centuries: Indians and Europeans in the American South, 1521–1704.* University of Georgia Press. p. 359.
13 McCartney, Martha W. and Lorena S. Walsh. 2003. *A Study of the Africans and African Americans on Jamestown Island and at Green Spring, 1619-1803,* Williamsburg: National Parks Service, p.15.

New Plymouth

The New England settlements followed the established European pattern of the time by declaring their right to settle the area on behalf of their government, in the English case, James I. The Mayflower passengers had gone armed, expecting conflict similar to that caused with the creation of the Jamestown Virginia colony. But European disease had already killed 90% of the Wampanoag people who had previously lived in the New Plymouth area. Therefore, unlike Jamestown, large scale military conflict between colonists and Indigenous people over land grabbing and forced labour did not occur for some time in the region around the new colony.

In the early 1620s the survival of the New Plymouth colony was initially very far from certain; in the first year of settlement half of the colonists died. Early problems included food, the fur trade and the threat of attack from neighbouring Indigenous Nations anxious about further colonist encroachments. The killing of six members (possibly more) of the Massachusetts Indigenous Nation at Wessagusset in 1623 especially stands out. It has been variously described as an early example of colonist trickery and manipulation leading to a massacre of Native Americans for their advantage[14] or a pre-emptive strike warding

Myles Standish

off an attack on the Plymouth and Wessagusset colonies[15]. Locally the attacks on the Wessagusset had the effect of establishing the reputation of the Mayflower colonists, and their military advisor Myles Standish in particular, as ruthless adversaries and survivors.

Indeed, both English mainland colonies did survive, and were soon joined by English Caribbean colonies - St. Kitts (1623), Barbados (1627), Nevis (1628), Providence (1630), Antigua (1632), Montserrat (1632), Anguilla (1650) and Jamaica in 1655, following the seizure of the island from the Spanish by

---

14 Jennings, F., 1976, *The Invasion of America: Indians, Colonialism and the Cant of Conquest'*, New York: Norton & Co., p.186.
15 Philbrick, N., 2007, *Mayflower: A Voyage to War*, London: Harper Perrenial.

English forces. The trade in African slaves, which had started in Jamestown in 1619, only became a feature of inter-colonial commerce involving New England after the colonists' war against the Pequot nation in 1636-8.

European colonization across the world from the late 15th to the 20th centuries took several distinct forms. But in North America and the Caribbean, English colonization was predominantly a mix in both time and location of two types of settlement. The first were colonies of white settlers who, having violently seized Indigenous land, grew to be the majority through the on-going clearance of the original inhabitants. The second type were built on land where European landowners, having cleared the area of its Native population, repopulated the territory with slaves seized from Africa.

The Swarming of the English

Although half of the Mayflower passengers were members of a distinct Puritan sect, the 'Separatists' (also sometimes referred to as 'Brownists'), the new region of English settlement in which they established their colony drew more mainstream Puritans and non-Puritan English settlers. One thousand colonists arrived in 1630 and a further 10,000 in the 1630s. By 1643 there were 20,000 settlers with an ever increasing need for land.[16] The establishment of the Massachusetts Bay Colony in 1630 under Governor John Winthrop, with a charter obtained from Charles I, can be seen as part of a wider British imperialist expansion into North America.

The rapid increase in the number of settlements resulted in unequal alliances between the different Puritan colonies, leading to the creation of the short-lived political entity known as the *United Colonies of New England* (UCNE 1643-84). The territory, influence, power and wealth of each colony changed over time. These shifts involved encroachment on neighbouring Indigenous Nations' land, and manipulation under colonial law of Native American ownership and rights to use their previously occupied territories. These early territorial manoeuvrings included the relationship between New Plymouth and the local Wampanoag Sachem, Massassoit, who had saved the Mayflower colonists in their first year of settlement. Though the relationship is often portrayed as between friends rather than a client one, New Plymouth colonists sought to control Massassoit's land holdings and sales.[17]

---

16 Calder, Angus,1998, *Revolutionary Empire: The Rise of the English-Speaking Empire from the Fifteenth Century to the 1780s*, London: Pimlico, p.124.
17 Jennings, 1976, *The Invasion of America*, pp.270 & 288-9.

The Pequot War

One result for the New Plymouth Colony settlers' 'alliance' with Massassoit was the neutrality of the Wampanoag in the *Pequot War* 1636/8. In May, 1637, John Mason was sent by the Connecticut Colony against the Pequot people. "*In a little more than One Hour, Five or Six Hundred Barbarians were dismissed from a world that was Burdened with them; not more than Seven or Eight persons escaping....*". The Pequots were defeated and hundreds of prisoners of war were sold into slavery to the West Indies. The Puritans saw the fate of the Pequots as an "act of God." Major Mason boasted that "*thus the Lord was pleased to smite our enemies in the hinder parts and to give us their land afor and inheritance*".[18] But some New England colonists were reluctant to retain Pequots as slaves in the region in which they had lived and rebelled, and so preferred to exchange some of them for enslaved Africans from the Caribbean.

Another of the leaders on the English side in the Pequot war, Captain John Underhill, was hired by the neighbouring Dutch Colonists in the early 1640s. His task was to undertake massacres against the Lunape Nations on Long Island, similar to those he had been part of in New England.[19] The Pequot massacres of 1637 had reverberated throughout the region and gave notice of future wars of annihilation to any Indigenous Nation contemplating resistance. For example, preparations for war in the early 1640s against the Narragansetts were made by New England colonial armies, including one led by the Mayflower passengers' military advisor, Myles Standish. Coming in the wake of the massacres of the Pequot, the mobilizations proved sufficient to drive the Narragansetts to temporarily accept tributary status.[20] This forced acquiescence for the Narragansetts, Wampanoag and other Southern New England nations was punctuated with challenges to colonist authority by different nations in 1653, 1660, and 1671. These confrontations resulted in further encroachments on 'Indian' lands and the imposition of fines and disarmaments by the colonists.[21]

---

18 Thomas, *Puritans, Indians, and the Concept of Race*, p.12-15, although Young, *Chronicles of the Pilgrim Fathers*, written in 1841, does tell the same story from Standish's perspective.
19 www.montaukwarrior.info/?page_id=277
20 Grenier, John, 2008, *The First Way of War: American War Making on the Frontier 1607 - 1814*, Cambridge: Cambridge University Press, p.29.
21 Newell, 2015, *Brethren by Nature*, p. 137.

King Philip's War

Finally, in 1675, against a background of inter-colony manoeuvring over land acquisition and enslavement of local Indigenous people, the actions of the New Plymouth Colony became the catalyst for 'King Philip's War'.[22] Hostilities had come to a head when three Wampanoags were hanged in Plymouth in 1675 for the murder of an Indian convert to Christianity, a so-called 'praying Indian', who was considered by his compatriots to be an informer and a collaborator. The Wampanoag were led by Massassoit's surviving son, Metacomet (known to the Europeans as 'King Philip'), in an alliance that included the Narragansetts, Nipmucks, Pocumtucks and other neighbouring Nations. Although the alliance gained some victories at first, the colonists recovered their military supremacy. This war officially ended in August 1676, shortly after Metacomet was captured and beheaded. The Puritans interpreted their victories as a sign of God's favour, but the Native-Americans who remained faced disease, cultural devastation, and the expropriation of their lands.[23]

However, *"No peace treaty was signed after August 12, and in many ways the fighting simply became less intense, less organised, and ... more distant from the area the war started in. Some scholars have argued that King Philip's War never ended because, in a figurative sense, it was the archetype of all Indian wars to follow"*.[24] By 1694, the New England authorities were offering a bounty for killing 'Hostile Indians', requiring their scalps as evidence.[25]

Those who surrendered in August 1676 were, like those in 1637, transported as slaves to the West Indies. *"...the sd heathen Malefactors men, women, and Children have been Sentenced & condemned to perpetuall Servitude and... Seventy of the sd Malefactors are transported in ths Ship – Sea-fflower"*.[26]

Some of the colonists, such as John Smith in Virginia, Myles Standish the Mayflower military advisor, John Mason of Connecticut and John Underhill in Massachusetts, had experience of the European wars of religion.[27] Consequently, settlers in the Americas in the late 16th and early 17th centuries

---

22 *ibid.* p. 134.
23 Foner and Garraty, *The Reader's Companion to American History* .
24 Lepore, Jill,1999, *The Name of War: King Philip's War and the Origins of American identity*, New York: Vintage Books.
25 Thomas, *Puritans, Indians, and the Concept of Race*, p.21.
26 *Slave certificate 12th September 1676* in Lepore,1999, *The Name of War*, p.163.
27 Grenier, 2008, *The First Way of War*, p.21.

were familiar with warfare that involved 'extravagant' violence against non-combatant populations as well as 'normal' fighting with other soldiers. The first English and Scots-Irish settler colonists in the Americas in the 17th century were also aware of the brutal tactics used in the settler colonization of Munster and Ulster. Moreover, the fraudulent administrative practices of land acquisition and distribution used in Ireland were well known to the senior figures who planned the Virginia colony, as several were also involved in the Plantation of Ulster. The wars against the local Indigenous Nations in North America in the 17th century, like later similar conflicts, were complex. The wars involved competing colonist groups, who manoeuvred to exercise influence and control over different Indigenous Nations and consequently created and exacerbated existing local grievances over land grabbing and enslavement.

Settlers in the two North American English colonial centres of Virginia and New England both engaged in massacres and wars with Indigenous Nations in the regions they sought to colonise. These early wars and attacks over the course of the 17th century established patterns of warfare that were emulated and developed by settlers over the next two hundred years of colonial incursion in new North American regions. The tactics used required the use of irregular forces, variously described as militias, rangers, wilderness fighters, etc., as well as regular troops. They also required making war on non-combatants both through direct assault and indirect attacks destroying or hampering supplies of food, burning crops and slaughtering or driving off livestock, sometimes known as 'feedfights'. The Tidewater raids (1644-46) in the Virginia region is an early example of colonist irregulars targeting food production and supplies as the means of driving out local Indigenous people. Attacks on food production and the deployment of irregulars in direct attack on non-combatants were also the military strategies used by the settler colonists in the Pequot War of 1636/8 and King Phillip's (Metacomet) War 1675-6. The defeat of Metacomet's forces did not so much end the New England wars between colonists and the Indigenous population as mark a new phase in the *Swarming of the English*.

Slavery and the Political Economy of New England

New England prides itself on its abolitionist heritage, but frequently ignores the role the region played in supplying the slave economy of the Caribbean and in organising the slave trade itself. Part of the growth of the economy of New England was the development of a textile industry that depended on slave produced cotton from the South. This, then, is the history of economic growth through genocide, slavery and slave trading which links the Caribbean and the North American Atlantic seaboard. Now that some New England institutions are starting to recognise their slave trading past, it is appropriate that a similar effort is made on the European side of the Atlantic.

The British North American colonies, including the West Indian islands, were part of a larger British Empire economy that was interdependent but with internal rivalries. Separate parts of the Empire had different interests but were dependent on the other colonies. Not all sections carried equal weight and, of course, the colonies were subordinate to the perceived political, diplomatic and economic interests of the metropolis. In particular, there was a very close economic relationship between the New England colonies and the West Indian slave-based sugar economy. The Caribbean islands found it more profitable to devote all their land to sugar production and import foodstuffs and other staples, while the New England colonies needed a Caribbean export market so that they could purchase manufactured goods from England. The devastating effect on the British West Indies of the 1776 rebellion against British colonialism in North America amply demonstrates the islands' dependence on trade with New England.[28]

The Puritans' Royal Charter

The perceived right of New Englanders to take over the lands of Indigenous Nations was implicit in the Puritans' Royal Charter, which granted authority for *'planting, ruling, order, and governing of New England in America, and to their successors and assignees forever'*. The Puritans professed that one of the reasons they came to New England was to convert the Native Americans to Christianity, and their charter stated that the purpose of their colonization was *"to incite the natives to the knowledge and obedience of the onlie true saviour of mankinde"*.[29] Not that the 'natives' were given a great deal

---

28 Carrington, Selwyn, "The American Revolution and the British West Indies' Economy", *The Journal of Interdisciplinary History, 17, no. 4 (1987).*, pp. 823–850.
29 'Charter of the Colony of the Massachusetts Bay in New England,' in Morgan, *The Founding of Massachusetts*, pp.303-330.

of choice in the matter. In 1646, the Court of Massachusetts decreed the death penalty for any, '*whether Christian or pagan,*' who would '*blaspheme his holy name, denying the true God, or his creation or government of the world, or shall curse God, or reproach the holy religion of God*'. During the same session the General Court forbade the Native-Americans the practice of their own religion.[30] Generally speaking, the Puritans held the Indigenous people in contempt and their Calvinism held that even those who had never seen a Bible nor heard the gospel were nevertheless damned. Meanwhile, the philosopher John Locke (1632 - 1704), sometimes referred to as 'The Father of Liberalism', wrote that hunters may justly be forced to alter their economy by an agricultural people.[31] This became part of a self-justification for expropriating the lands of the Indigenous population. As Matthew Parker put it: '*Natives were part of the landscape rather than the owners of it*'.[32]

However, the first Puritan settlers, the Mayflower passengers at Plymouth colony, would clearly not have survived their first winter without the help of the Wampanoag people of the region. Nevertheless, conflict with the Indigenous population was inevitable as a result of radically different customs and practices of land ownership.

When the so-called 'Pilgrim Fathers' arrived in 1620, they did not bring any slaves with them, but they did bring the biblical justification for slavery. Slavery, they maintained, was established by the law of God in Israel and, regarding themselves as the Elect of God, New Englanders looked upon the enslavement of the Indians and Negroes as a "sacred privilege Divine Providence was pleased to grant His chosen people".[33] Were not 'Negroes' and 'Indians' infidels beyond the pale of civil and spiritual rights as heathen people whose souls were damned to eternal perdition?[34]

African enslavement and New England

The first reliable reference to African enslavement within New England is in 1638, when the governor, John Winthrop speaks of the return to Boston of

---

30 Thomas, *Puritans, Indians, and the Concept of Race,* p.5.
31 Calder, Angus, *Revolutionary Empire,* p.202-3.
32 Parker, Matthew, 2011, *The Sugar Barons: Family, Corruption, Empire and War,* London: Hutchinson, p.19.
33 Mather, Cotton, 1706, *The Negro Christianized: An Essay to Excite and Assist that Good Work, the Instruction of Negro-Servants in Christianity,* Boston: Green, p.2.
34 Greene, Lorenzo, 1942, *The Negro in Colonial New England, 1620-1776.* New York: Columbia University Press, p.61.

Captain William Pierce in the Salem ship, *Desire*. It had gone to Providence Island in the Caribbean with a cargo including some captive Pequot people from the war of 1637 who he had sold into slavery there. The *Desire* returned with a cargo of 'salt, cotton, tobacco and Negroes'.[35]

Article 91 of the Massachusetts 'Body of Liberties' from 1641 reads as follows:

> *It is Ordered by this Court and the Authority thereof; That there shall never be any Bond-slavery, Villenage or Captivity amongst us, unless it be lawful Captives taken in just Wars, and such strangers as willingly sell themselves or are sold to us, and such shall have the Liberties and Christian usage which the Law of God established in Israel concerning such persons doth morally require; Provided this exempts none from servitude who shall be judged thereto by Authority.*[36]

At first glance, a ruling against slavery, until one reads the exemptions: *'lawful Captives taken in just Wars'* and *'such strangers as ... are sold to us'*. So, in 1645, Emanuel Downing, in a letter to his brother in law, Governor John Winthrop, urging a war with the Narragansett people, wrote:

> *If upon a Just warre the Lord should deliver them into our hands, wee might easily have men woemen and children enough to exchange for Moores ... I suppose you know verie well how wee shall mayneteyne 20 Moores cheaper than one Englishe servant.*[37]

In New England, the African slave population was small compared to the slave-based plantation system that developed in Southern mainland and Caribbean colonies. However, numbers fluctuated and included periods in the 18th century where substantial slave plantations thrived in areas such as Rhode Island. But Rhode Island in the 18th century was better known as a shipping centre for the slave trade, mostly carrying slaves between Africa and the Caribbean. New England slave trading and related financial and trading activities had grown from small beginnings in Massachusetts in the late 1630s. The establishment in the New England colonies of slave populations was

---

35 Winthrop, John, 1908, *Winthrop's journal : "History of New England", 1630-1649*, New York: Scribner, p.260.
36 Von Frank, Albert J. 1994, "John Saffin: Slavery and Racism in Colonial Massachusetts." *Early American Literature* 29, no. 3, p.259.
37 Jordan, Winthrop, 1961, "The Influence of the West Indies on the Origins of New England Slavery." *The William and Mary Quarterly* 18, no. 2, p.244.

initially through enslavement of Indigenous people captured in war or trapped by legal manipulation. Some Indigenous slaves were not kept in the region but were exported to the slave markets of the Caribbean.

While there was a shortage of labour in New England, the land was not generally suitable for the kind of cash-crop agriculture to which slavery is most suited, although, the Narragansett area of Rhode Island developed its own plantation system, using slave labour on estates dedicated to raising horses, cattle, and dairy cows. There were at least ten plantations in Narragansett that ranged in size from 1,000 to 5,000 acres, each employing between ten and twenty slaves.[38] But this was not the norm, and slavery in New England was a predominantly small-scale, urban institution and, at the first census of New England's population in 1715, there were 158,000 Europeans to 4,150 Africans.[39] Some of the European population were indentured labourers, working within a system of unfree labour that caused them to be bound by a contract to work for a particular master for a fixed time period. There were 18 such indentured labourers on the Mayflower and 180 were sent over to the Massachusetts Bay colony at its foundation. A food shortage meant that they could not earn their keep and in 1630 those who had survived were freed. Whether they then starved to death in their new condition is not recorded.[40] Slavery and other forms of unfree labour were to disappear in New England not because of any exalted moral objection to the holding of human beings as chattel, but because it did not pay.

> *An early realization that the price of Negroes also was greater than the worth of their labour under ordinary circumstances in New England led the Yankee participants in the African trade to market their slave cargoes in the plantation colonies instead of bringing them home.*[41]

A division of labour developed among the Puritans in the American colonies, with those who went to the Caribbean specialising in cash-crop plantations and those in New England supplying, servicing and trading with

38 Farrow, Anne; Lang, Joel and Frank, Jenifer, 2008, *Complicity: How the North Promoted, Prolonged, and Profited from Slavery*, New York: Ballantine, p.77; Greene, Lorenzo, 1928, "Slave-Holding New England and Its Awakening." *The Journal of Negro History* 13, no. 4, p.513.
39 Greene, *The Negro in Colonial New England*, p.75.
40 Thomas Dudley, 'Letter to the Countess of Lincoln', in Young, *Chronicles of the First Planters of Massachusetts Bay*, p. 312.
41 Phillips, Ulrich, 1918, *American Negro Slavery: A Survey of the Supply, Employment and Control of Negro Labor as Determined by the Plantation Régime*, New York: Appleton, p.101

them. In 1630, while some Puritans led by John Winthrop were voyaging to their 'City upon a Hill' in Massachusetts, another group of several hundred took over the island of Old Providence lying off the coast of Nicaragua. These Puritans in the Caribbean were funded by the Earl of Warwick, who had landed the first cargo of African slaves in Virginia in 1619.[42] With the establishment of New Providence, African slaves were imported there too. Indeed, importation was so rapid that the outnumbered Puritans became apprehensive of rebellion, with good cause as it turned out. Numbers of the enslaved escaped to live as maroons in the hills and staged a concerted uprising in 1638. This was defeated, but so weakened the colonists that the Spanish were easily able to reconquer the island in 1638.[43] Thereafter, Puritans in the Caribbean joined the mainstream British colonies, relying on their greater defensive protection.

One of the first settlers in Barbados was Henry Winthrop, son of the future Governor of Massachusetts Bay colony. In 1628 he had sent a crop of tobacco back to his father in London. But the tobacco from Barbados was of poor quality and the transformation of Barbados into a sugar plantation economy would have to wait until the 1640s.[44] The Winthrop family correspondence goes a long way to explaining the early English colonization project in the Americas. Certainly, Puritan religious principles were important, but these did not in any way inhibit the desire or ability to make a profit, and slavery was the most profitable way to do so. In 1645, John Winthrop's nephew wrote to his uncle from Barbados to say that the island's planters had bought 'a thousand Negroes; and the more thay buy, the better able they are to buy, for in a year and a half they will earn (with God's blessing) as much as they cost'.[45]

New England and the Slave Trade

While the actual practice of chattel slavery was not a success in New England, slavery in the West Indies became essential to the economy of the North American colonies. Once the fur trade had been exhausted by over hunting, New England had nothing to trade for manufactured goods which could be produced cheaper in England. However, they were able to find a market for their horses, timber, candle oil, flour, dried fish and barrels in the West Indies. In 1641, John Winthrop wrote 'These straits set our people on work to provide fish, clapboards, planks etc. ... and to look to the West Indies

---

42 Calder, *Revolutionary Empire*, p.135.
43 Phillips, *American Negro Slavery*, p.99.
44 Parker, *The Sugar Barons*, pp.17, 35-37.
45 Farrow et al, *Complicity*, p.70-72.

for a trade'. Richard Vines, a Puritan doctor from New England who was working in Barbados wrote to John Winthrop in 1647: '*Men are so intent upon planting sugar that they would rather buy foode at very deare rates than produce it by labour, soe infinite is the profitt of sugar'.*[46] Samuel Winthrop who, as a child, had sailed with his father on the voyage to found the Massachusetts Bay colony in 1630, set himself up as a merchant in Antigua and St Kitts trading between the Caribbean, New England and the 'Wine Islands', as the Canaries and the Azores were known. There, importing goods and serving as agent for shippers in England and New England, he raised sufficient capital to purchase land and become a planter. One of the first there to switch to large-scale sugar production, he shipped over 20,000 pounds of sugar a year by the early 1660s. When he died he had over 1,000 acres and sixty-four slaves, and owned a quarter of the island, Barbuda.[47]

The first voyage between the Bay Colony and Barbados set sail in September 1641, although it took nearly a year to return. Despite the dangers, by 1647 there was a regular trade between Barbados and the northern colonies which found in the sugar islands a market for their surplus agricultural production. This was also to the advantage of the plantation owners for, while New England produce was expensive, it was still cheaper and more reliable than imports from Europe. This trade expanded to the extent that, in the late 1660s, between 35 and 65 vessels a year from Boston, Salem and Newport arrived in Bridgetown, Barbados. John Sanford, founder of the Portsmouth colony on Rhode Island and Governor of Newport, sent his son Peleg Sanford to Barbados to act as the agent for Rhode Island. He prospered in the trade, returning eventually to become Governor of Rhode Island itself in the early 1680s, by which time the West Indian trade had become the cornerstone of New England commerce involving half the ships entering and leaving Boston.

This trade, aided by co-religionist and family contacts, led Boston and the nearby town of Salem, along with Newport on Rhode Island, to embark on an ambitious programme of ship-building; a 300-ton ship was built in Salem as early as 1641. John Winthrop himself financed the construction of the Massachusetts Bay Colony's first ship, the *Blessing of the Bay*, launched in

46 Parker, *The Sugar Barons* p.35-6.
47 Gragg, Larry D. 1993, "A Puritan in the West Indies: The Career of Samuel Winthrop." *The William and Mary Quarterly,* 50, no. 4, pp.771-4.

1631. By 1700, Boston and nearby towns were turning out 70 ships a year - the most in number and tonnage in the Western Hemisphere.

> *American-built ships not only dominated the West Indian and Coastwise trades, where they accounted respectively for 96 percent and 93 percent of the ships, but were even important in the shipping coming directly from Africa. On this route, they accounted for 44 percent of the ships, with English-built ships making up the rest.[48]*

Of course the *'shipping coming directly from Africa'* was full of enslaved people.

Triangular Trades

Trade with the colonies in North America was an important market for British manufactured goods while, in turn, the New England economy evolved so that these purchases of British manufactured products were financed by the trade with the West Indies. It is common to talk of the 'Triangular Trade'. This is usually understood to be between the English slave trading ports such as Liverpool, Bristol or London, then south to the West Coast of Africa with manufactured items to be exchanged for enslaved people. The slaves were then carried across the Atlantic to the Caribbean or the area that was to become the Southern states of the USA, then back to England with sugar, cotton and other plantation crops. However, it is probably more accurate to talk of the 'Triangular Trades', plural, as another important triangle went from New England to West Africa with rum, which could be traded for captives in Africa. These slaves could be exchanged for molasses in the West Indies to supply the rum distilling industry in New England. A slave, who could be purchased in Africa for an amount of rum that cost £2 or £3 to produce in North America, could be sold for between £30 and £80 in Barbados or the southern mainland colonies.[49] These enormous quantities of alcohol had the added advantage, from the slave-traders' point of view, of setting in train a destabilising epidemic of alcoholism in Africa that vastly increased levels of violence, broke down traditional relationships and thereby facilitated slave-taking. As Boston, Salem and Nantucket became the pre-eminent slaving ports in the region, the distillation of millions of gallons of rum for the slave-trade made this the largest

48 Klein, Herbert, 1978, *The Middle Passage: Comparative Studies in the Atlantic Slave Trade,* Princeton: Princeton University Press, pp.133-4.
49 Greene, *The Negro in Colonial New England*, pp.30-31.

manufacturing industry in New England. By the Eighteenth Century, Rhode Island had thirty distilleries and Massachusetts had sixty-three, producing five million gallons of rum a year.[50]

The first slave trading vessel from New England to Barbados landed in 1643 and the 18th century saw the rise of the New England Colonies as slave-carriers rather than direct exploiters of slave-labour.

> *Quick to see the unprofitableness of the Negro slave as a laborer in such an environment, when the price of the slave was greater than the labor returned, the ingenious Yankee soon found a market in the West Indies for slaves, exchanged for rum, sugar and molasses on the Guinea Coast. Massachusetts early assumed a commanding position in this trade. The ports of Boston and Salem prospered especially. Their merchants carried on a "brisk trade to Guinea" for many years, marketing most of their slaves in the West Indies.[51]*

Subsequently, however, the slave trade of Rhode Island outstripped that of Massachusetts. This not only played a vital role in maintaining and enabling the expansion of the slave-based plantation system in the British Caribbean, but also underpinned the creation of a New England mercantile oligarchy through the fortunes which this commerce generated. It also funded the foundation of many prestigious universities. A recent book published by Rutgers University outlining the relationship between the university and slavery, calls colleges 'tools of empire', part of the colonial garrison.

> *Though just a preliminary investigation, eight months of arduous archival research have confirmed our suspicions that Rutgers University and its founders and benefactors were prodigiously involved in the slave trade and the slavery economy. Albeit indirectly, we know the college benefited from Native American Removal, breaking ground in a land once occupied by the Lenni Lenape. We know that our namesake, Henry Rutgers, was a slave owner. We know the Livingston Campus is named after William Livingston, whose family was involved in the slave trade and were well-known slave owners. We know that the early financial*

---

50 Bailey, Ronald, 1990, "The Slave(ry) Trade and the Development of Capitalism in the United States: The Textile Industry in New England." *Social Science History* 14, no. 3, p.385.
51 Greene, *Slave-Holding New England*, pp.496-8.

health of our institution was largely a result of monetary and in-kind contributions from individuals who made their wealth off of slaves.[52]

This reliance on the slave trade and the West Indian slave economy persisted up to the 13 colonies' struggle for independence in the latter part of the 18th century.

The effects of this slave trade were manifold. On the eve of the American Revolution it formed the very basis of the economic life of New England; about it revolved, and on it depended, most of her industries. The vast sugar, molasses and rum trade, shipbuilding, the distilleries, a great many of the fisheries, the employment of artisans and seamen, even agriculture - all were dependent on the slave traffic.[53]

The Declaration of Independence

One of the many factors behind the declaration of Independence by the 13 North American colonies was the way in which the proposed duties on molasses and sugar in the Sugar Act of 1764 would "*ruin fisheries cause the destruction of the rum distilleries and destroy the slave trade*". The Massachusetts merchants asserted that the "*destruction of the Negro commerce would throw 5000 seamen out of employment and would cause 700 ships to rot in idleness on their wharves*".[54] The Rhode Island merchants made similar claims. Even allowing for exaggeration, this demonstrates the importance of slavery to the New England economy at the time of the War of Independence.[55]

At the outbreak of the US War of Independence, Rhode Island controlled two-thirds or more of the colonies' slave trade with Africa. When the trade resumed after the war, Rhode Island resumed its predominance, shipping nearly 50,000 new slaves in less than twenty years.[56]

Though New England's slave population was relatively small, African American and Indigenous American slaves were part of the North Eastern states for well over a hundred years from the late 17th century. Moreover, slave trading through ports in New England from then to the late 18th century, though

---

52 Fuentes, Marisa J. and White, Deborah Gray (Eds.), 2016, *Scarlet and Black: Slavery and Dispossession in Rutgers History,* New Brunswick: Rutgers University Press.
53 Greene, *The Negro in Colonial New England,* pp.68-9.
54 *A Statement of the Massachusetts Trade and Fisheries.*
55 Bailey, *The Slave(ry) Trade and the Development of Capitalism in the United States,* p.374.
56 Farrow, Lang and Frank, *Complicity,* p.121.

small compared with elsewhere in the Americas, was substantial. Even following the formal outlawing of the slave-trade by the US government, many New England businessmen were deeply involved in the illegal trade, shipping the enslaved from Africa to Cuba, where many Northerners owned sugar and coffee plantations. The most famous of these was James DeWolf of Rhode Island, whose family owned six Cuban plantations as part of a commercial empire that included banking, shipping, land speculation and textile production. The shipping interests included the illegal slave trade. When he was elected to the US Senate for Rhode Island, it coincided with the conviction of a slave trader in Boston. The Salem Gazette said: "*Thus one Slave Trader goes into the United States Senate, and another into the State's prison*".

While differences over slavery were fudged in the Declaration of Independence and the US Constitution, the economic development of the Northern states continued to be intertwined with the slave-based South. In 1786, the Cabot brothers, having made their fortunes in the slave trade, established the first cotton mill in the Americas. But it was the invention of the cotton gin by Eli Whitney in 1793 that made the mass production of cotton fabric practical, as the separation of cotton fibre and seed was now mechanised. Total US consumption of raw cotton increased from five million pounds in 1790 to 470 million pounds by 1860.[57] Despite many Northern textile mill owners purporting to abhor slavery and some historians trying to separate the production of the finished product from the production of the raw material by forced labour, the profits of the process clearly depended on the unremunerated labour of the enslaved.[58] Of course technological change was responsible for the vastly increased productivity in the manufacture of cotton textiles, but industrialisation did nothing to lighten the workload of the slaves, rather it made matters worse since slaves were driven harder to keep up with the steam-driven processing of the harvested sugar cane. Slaves worked under drivers in gangs that would build up a fierce momentum. Modern "human resources" techniques, such as speed-up and measured task working, enforced by the whip and other torture, pushed a cotton-picking productivity increase of 400% between 1800 and 1860 in the USA.[59]

---

57 Bailey, Ronald, 1994, "The Other Side of Slavery: Black Labor, Cotton, and Textile Industrialization in Great Britain and the United States." *Agricultural History, Vol. 68, no. 2*, p.46.
58 Genovese, Eugene, 1971, *In Red and Black: Marxian explorations in Southern and Afro-American History*, Knoxville: University of Tennessee Press.

But the economy of New England was not only dependent on the supply of cheap and plentiful raw cotton. The production of poor quality 'Negro Cloth' for slave clothing was vital to the continued operation of Northern textile mills during times of economic crisis.[60] Equally, capital investment by the New England banks became essential to the development of Southern slave-based cotton agriculture, with mortgages frequently secured on the ownership of the enslaved. By the middle of the 19th century, the two million slaves represented a billion dollars in credit.

From the earliest European settlement until the final end of slavery, New England was enmeshed in slavery, albeit at arms' length. The selling of Pequot prisoners of war into Caribbean slavery, was merely the first move in the process. Food and other supplies from New England were essential to the profitability of West Indian sugar slavery, and New England rum became one of the main 'currencies' in the transatlantic slave-trade.   The attributing of the Pilgrim Fathers as the originators of the democratic tradition of the United States, on deeper examination demonstrates that US and British political traditions are soundly founded on slavery, racism and genocide.

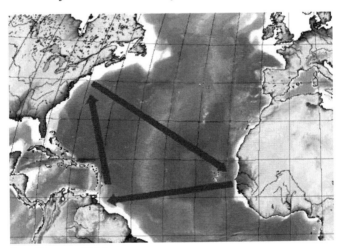

Rum, Slaves and Molasses

59 Baptist, Edward, 2015, *The Half Has Never Been Told*, New York: Basic Books, pp.164, 332, 426.
60 Ogden, Nancy, Catherine Perkins, and David M. Donahue, 2008, "Not a Peculiar Institution: Challenging Students' Assumptions about Slavery in U.S. History." *The History Teacher* 41, no. 4, p.470.

Settler Colonialism Post-Seventeenth Century

"No Savage should inherit the land" [61]

The establishment of America's first "Ranger" force towards the ending of King Philip's War of 1675-76 fed into wars against ongoing Native resistance. Ranger numbers grew with the spread of the practice of offering state sponsored scalp bounties, and the rangers were important in the early 18th century wars in New England in establishing extermination practices. [62] The story of the relationships in the 18th and 19th centuries between Indigenous peoples and the British and French, and, after 1776, American colonial expansionists, is a tale of wars. Though there were wars directly between colonists and Indigenous Nations, in addition there was deliberate involvement by the European powers of different Indigenous Nations at different times in intercolonial wars. 1689-98 The Nine-Years' War between European powers was known in the Americas as King William's War, and involved both the Caribbean Islands and territories in what are now the USA and Canada. Queen Anne's War (1702–1713) and King George's War (1744-48) were the names given to those parts of The War of the Spanish Succession and The War of the Austrian Succession fought in North America. The French and Indian War (1754 - 63) yet again involved the recruitment and manipulation of different Indigenous Nations by the English and French colonial powers as they fought each other and Indigenous Nation allies. These wars often included the pattern of brutal land grabbing pioneered by the English in the 17th century and were not always restricted to wars with the French. For example, English and Scottish Rangers were used in what the British then formally considered Spanish Florida, in the establishment of the colony of Georgia in the 1730s in the face of resistance from the Cherokee Nation and Maroon communities.

Irregular forces had become a feature of British colonial settlement in the 17th century, and the continued use of such militia irregulars during both the British colonial and United States phases, became mixed in with the process of the establishment of new colonial settlements. Small holding settlers were frequently obliged to sell their holdings to larger wealthier and expanding landlords. The result was that newer European colonists were often joined by

---

61 General Bradock to Shingas, a leader of the Delaware (Lenape) people 1755. Quoted in Gott, Richard, 2011, *Britain's Empire*, London, Verso, p.16.
62 Grenier, 2008, *The First Way of War*, pp.33, 39 & 52.

older colonists who were pushed out from the older North Atlantic coastal settlements, and both groups violently took new areas of Indigenous territory, destroying the livelihoods of Indigenous peoples in the process.[63]

Extermination

The key aim in the so called Indian Wars, starting with those along the Atlantic Seaboard in the 17th century, was the acquisition of territory designated "Indian", by forcing indigenous populations to move west, south or north. These wars involved large-scale killing. In the 1763 Pontiac's Rebellion, the English Major General, Jeffery Amherst, made this clear when he wrote to Colonel Bouquet, a subordinate officer, "*Could it not be contrived to send the Small Pox among those disaffected tribes of Indians?*".[64] In 1867, the future US Army commanding general, William T Sherman, advocated that "*we must act with vindictive earnestness against the Sioux, even to their extermination, men, women and children*".[65]

But the reductions of populations of Indigenous Nations were engineered only partly through direct military attacks. Expansion of colonist settlements also involved new variations in *low intensity tactics*; for example, the slaughter of herds of buffalo in the third quarter of the 19th century, on which the Indigenous Nations of the Plains had come to depend. However, to understand this later phase under an independent colonial USA in the expulsion, genocide, settlement cycles, it is necessary to briefly trace events in the late 18th century.

In October 1763 English colonial expansion was formally limited by proclamation by the English Crown, following British success in the French and Indian War.[66] By implication, with this proclamation of settlement limitation, the Crown was laying claim to sovereignty to vast areas, then still not colonised, in the west of what is now known as Canada and the USA. In addition, in 1765 the English Parliament sought to reinforce these limitations to settlement which were being ignored by the colonists, with troops paid for through the introduction of a Stamp Act, that imposed a tax on the colonists' printed materials. This led to the rebels' slogan "taxation without representation is tyranny". By trying to confine his colonial settler subjects to the Atlantic

---

63 Horne, Gerald, 2018, *The Apocalypse of Settler Colonialism: The Roots of Slavery, White Supremacy, and Capitalism in Seventeenth-Century North America and the Caribbean*, New York: Monthly Review.
64 Quoted in Gott, Richard, 2011, *Britain's Empire*, London, Verso, p.28.
65 Quoted in Cozzens, Peter, 2016, *The Earth is Weeping*, London: Atlantic Books, p. 106.
66 Gott, 2011, *Britain's Empire*, p.37.

coastal territories, and denying them the westward expansion they sought, George III unwittingly encouraged rebellion and the transformation of the early 13 colonies into the USA in 1776. The American Revolution was both against the Crown and for colonist expansion into the territories of the Indigenous Nations of the Delaware, Cherokee, Muskogee, Seneca, Mohawk, Shawnee, and Miami.

> In the 1776-83 period, *The rebel forces were met with resistance movements and confederations identified with leaders such as Buckongeahelas of the Delaware; Alexander McGillivray of the Muskogee-Creek; Little Turtle and Blue Jacket of the Miami-Shawnee alliance; Joseph Brant of the Mohawk; and Cornplanter of the Seneca; as well as the great Tecumseh and the Shawnee-led confederation in the Ohio Valley. Without their sustained resistance, the intended genocide would have been complete.*[67]

The End of the Revolutionary War

The British, having refocused their colonization plans to South East Asia, conceded defeat in the American revolution in 1783 to the US rebels. The US Government now not only inherited the Atlantic coastal states territorial area but also the right to claim the regions designated as under the sovereignty of the British Crown in the 1763 proclamation. The new independent Government was now free to create a colonization procedure involving military occupation of the land of the Indigenous Nations under the *Northwest Ordinance* of 1787. In 1790 this was followed by the Six statutes, known as the *Non-intercourse Act*, which imposed what proved to be very temporary new limitation to settler expansion into the territories of Indigenous Nations.[68]

The early organization of the New England and Virginia settlements had provided the military model for the territorial wars against Indigenous Nations, up to and including those of the late 18th and early 19th centuries. In the "Indian Wars" that took place at the same time as the American Revolution, 1774-83, "we find the same elements - necessity and efficiency, the uncontrollable momentum of extravagant violence, and the quest for the subjugation of Indians - that had defined the first way of war throughout the

---

67 Dunbar-Ortiz, Roxanne, 2018, "Loaded: a disarming history of the second amendment", *Monthly Review*, Jan 2018, p.26.
68 Cozzens, 2016, *The Earth is Weeping*, p.13.

colonial period".[69] Major General 'Mad' Anthony Wayne, continued adopting these tactics with the formation of the US regular army in the 1790s. Wayne "also knew to strike directly at the Indians' points of greatest vulnerability: their villages, fields, and non-combatants".[70] Both colonial militia irregular forces and regular US federal troops who they supplemented, now acted in concert.

Local militia had been established by English colonisers from the beginning of the 17th century. However, with the Second Amendment contained in the Bill of Rights of 1791, "*A well-regulated Militia, being necessary to the security of a free State...*" was enshrined in the US Constitution. The militias had, long before independence, added the role of slave catcher to that of "Indian fighter". Both roles required that, for settlers to become militiamen, they needed to be armed. The Second Amendment's supplementary provision of the Right to Bear Arms was a progression of the requirement of the very early colonial governments that colonists be armed.[71]

19th Century Colonial Expansion

In 1803 Napoleon Bonaparte sold the Louisiana territory of 828,000 square miles (2,144,520 square km) claimed by France to the US Government, which doubled the size of the United States. The Louisiana Purchase, together with the establishment of the USA/Canada border in 1818 and the sale of the Floridas by Spain in 1819 gave notice of forthcoming expansion plans into the territories of a large number of Indigenous Nations. The Louisiana Purchase alone included the area later designated *Indian Territory* plus the territories of a number of Indigenous Nations including: Sioux, Cheyenne, Arapaho, Crow, Pawnee, Osage, Comanche.[72] The wars of the 1790s, such as The Ohio Indian War (1790-1795) were soon to be followed by others, The Northwest Indian War (1810 -1813) and The Creek War (1813-1814), at the end of which Major General Andrew Jackson demanded 23 million acres as war reparations.[73]

In 1817 President James Monroe told Jackson, that, "*the savage requires a greater extent of territory to sustain it than is compatible with the progress and just claims of civilized life, and must yield to it*".[74] In 1823 Monroe outlined the

69 Grenier, 2008, *The First Way of War*, p.147.
70 *ibid.*, p.203.
71 Dunbar-Ortiz, Roxanne, 2014, *An Indigenous Peoples' History of the United States*, Boston, USA, Beacon Press, p.29.
72 *ibid.*, p.95.
73 Grenier, 2008, *The First Way of War*, p.204.
74 Cozzens, 2016, *The Earth is Weeping*, p.14.

Monroe Doctrine that the Western Hemisphere was closed to future colonization by European powers. However, he left it to Jackson, when he became President, to implement this *yielding* of territory policy, now limited to the USA only, using new regulations such as the Removal Act of 1830. This policy led to the forced transfer of thousands of Indigenous people, in the course of which 50% of those forcibly relocated died; and yet more wars against Indigenous Nations, both official and unofficial. 'Frustrated by continued Indian resistance and befuddled how best to quash it, the Army looked the other way when either its own men or citizens acting on its name subjected Seminoles, Arapahos, Cheyennes, and Sioux to the same treatment that earlier Americans had inflicted on Abenakis, Cherokees, and even Christian Indians.'[75]

California: "Utter Extermination" General Sherman[76]

In 1848 the USA victory in the war with Mexico over Texas annexation also led to the acquisition of an additional 525,000 square miles to its territory. This including the land that makes up all or parts of present-day Arizona, Colorado, Nevada, New Mexico, Utah, Wyoming and California. "US occupation and settlement exterminated more than one hundred thousand California Native people in twenty-five years, reducing the population to thirty thousand by 1870 - quite possibly the most extreme demographic disaster of all time".[77]

In the period 1846-1873 there were some 370 massacres in California.[78] In the second half of the 19th century, although military force and confinement was met with armed resistance, large scale rapid population decline of Indigenous people continued.

Native population USA: 1850 - 365000; 1890 - 228000

The data is conclusive, nearly three quarters of the decline in population can be attributed to westward expansion.[79]

"By the 1890s, although some military assaults on Indigenous communities and valiant Indigenous armed resistance continued, most of the surviving

75 Grenier, 2005, *The First Way of War*, p.222.
76 Madley, Benjamin, 2016, *An American Genocide, The United States and the California Catastrophe, 1846-1873*, London, Yale University Press, p.342.
77 Dunbar-Ortiz, 2014, *An Indigenous Peoples' History*, p.129.
78 Madley, 2016, *An American Genocide*.
79 https://nativestudy.wordpress.com

Indigenous refugees were confined to federal reservations, their children transported to distant boarding schools to unlearn their Indigenousness".[80]

In the late 19th century, with the passing of a series of laws such as the General Allotment Act in 1887 and the Curtis Act of 1898, the loss of territory of the Indigenous Nations greatly increased, despite treaties stating the contrary. The new laws created two categories of what had been designated Indian Territory: *allotted* and *unassigned*. The total of allotments made to individual indigenous people left most of the Indian Territory unassigned and available for settlers to purchase or otherwise acquire. Land designated as "Indian" decreased from 156 million acres in 1881 to 50 million acres in 1934, when the Indian Reorganisation Act was passed.

In the case of the Osage Nation, attempts at acquisition by outsiders of land that had been "allotted" to Osage tribal members led to widespread violence. Having been forcibly moved several times in the 19th century, in 1907 the Osage found themselves only allocated barren land plots in what became Oklahoma State. However, they retained mineral rights as a tribe, and oil was struck on their land. In the 1920s, though tribal wealth was legally established, control over Osage wealth was in the hands of the Bureau of Indian Affairs, which locally meant prominent white citizens of Osage County, including the soon to be notorious figure of William Hale. Recent research has exposed a string of Hale's legal and medical frauds, intimidation, robberies and murders against Osage tribal members, known locally as the Reign of Terror. Most shocking is the revelation of large numbers of earlier murders unrelated to Hale in the Osage area. A prominent member of the Osage tribe is quoted in describing one of the court cases that followed the terror by saying, "*It is a question in my mind whether the jury [all white] is considering a murder case or not. The question for them to decide is whether a white man killing an Osage is murder – or merely cruelty to animals*".[81]

'Extravagant violence' is very much a legacy of the Mayflower journey. Yet, in the commemorations of the last 400 years, it has been omitted.

---

80 Dunbar-Ortiz, 2014, An Indigenous Peoples' History, p.153.
81 Grann, David, 2017, *Killers of the Flower Moon: Oil, Money, Murder and the Birth of the FBI*, London: Simon & Schuster.

The Telling of the Mayflower Story - A Brief History

> *"... some will say, what right have I to go live in the heathen's country?...... the land of America from the Cape de Florida unto the Bay of Canada ..... is proper to the King of England ..."*

These extracts are taken from the promotional part of what is known as Mourt's Relations, first published in England in 1622. Most of the booklet was probably drafted in late 1621 by some of the Mayflower Separatists' leaders. This account was soon supplemented by others such as Edward Winslow's *Good News from New England* published in 1624. William Bradford's *Of Plymouth Plantation* was not published until 1856 in Boston, but soon became the most famous of the on-the-spot Mayflower accounts and an important source for historical research. However, from its beginning in 1622 the Mayflower Story has been used primarily for political purposes, with history continuing to be intertwined with the ideology and events of the day.

Plymouth Rock became a symbol for the English colonists in 1741. But with the inauguration of Forefathers Day in 1769 in Plymouth Massachusetts, the commemorations were repurposed. The start of the War of Independence/American Revolution in 1775 was only six years away, and marking the establishment of the Plymouth settlement became mixed up with political discontent and divisions among English settlers over colonial government. Even "the story of King Philip's War [was employed] as a propaganda tool against the British".[82] Central to the rebels' arguments was the inadequacy of the British Crown's conduct of war against the Indigenous peoples of North America. Reference is explicit in the US's Declaration of Independence:

> *"He [The King of Great Britain, George III] ... has endeavoured to bring on the inhabitants of our frontiers, the merciless Indian Savages, whose known rule of warfare, is an undistinguished destruction of all ages, sexes and conditions".[83]*

Subsequently, the revival in the early 1790s of *Forefathers Day* on 22-23 December was now part of patriotism in an independent USA. As part of this independence came the issue of fighting the "Indians"; something that was recalled when it was time to commemorate the Pilgrim Fathers:

---

82 Lepore, 1999, *The Name of War*, p.177.
83 From the *Declaration of Independence*, 4th July 1776.

We have come to this Rock, to record here our homage for our Pilgrim Fathers ... they encountered the dangers of ... the violence of savages ... We feel that we are on the spot where the first scene of our history was laid ... and civilization, and letters made their first lodgement in a vast extent of country, covered with a wilderness, and peopled by roving barbarians.[84]

No mention of the events of 1620, the Mayflower or the beginning of the Plymouth Colony was made in the declaration of Thanksgiving Day as a National holiday in 1863. However, Abraham Lincoln's proclamation, coming as it did during the American Civil War, served, in the aftermath of the war, to identify the Union's cause with the notion that the roots of the USA lie in the Thanksgiving of 1621.

Against a background of Indian Wars elsewhere in the expanding USA, Plymouth Rock was given its own canopy in 1867 in time for the 250th anniversary in 1870. Though soon to be Vice-President, Henry Wilson, made no reference in his speech to indigenous Americans, he did find *"in the cabin of the Mayflower the foundations of civil liberty in America"*. At these commemorations Wilson claimed that the example of the Pilgrims provided inspiration for the American Revolution, freedom of the press, the right of petition, the emancipation of the slaves and the right of men to vote.[85]

300th year Anniversary

In the next 50 years the Mayflower became a part of politicking in the USA, with events such as the formal recognition by Massachusetts State of Forefathers Day in 1895 further institutionalising the commemorations. By the tercentenary of 1920, presidents and other prominent politicians regularly made reference to the Mayflower journey, Pilgrims, 1620 and Thanksgiving. A Mayflower ship built in 1896, was converted in 1905 from a light warship to the presidential yacht and used in 1921 to bring President Warren G Harding to Plymouth Massachusetts for the largest commemoration to date, the tercentenary. The great and good dedicated parks, new constructions and themselves to the memory of the Pilgrims and what they had achieved. The

---

84 From the oration delivered at Plymouth, Massachusetts, 22nd December 1820 by Daniel Webster, orator, lawyer, US Senator and Secretary of State.
85 Pilgrim Society, 1871, *The Proceedings at the celebration by the Pilgrim Society at Plymouth: December 21, 1870 of the two hundred and fiftieth anniversary of the landing of the pilgrims*, Plymouth, Mass: John Wilson Press, p.130.

political establishment in the USA, in the course of the late 19th and 20th centuries, mixed up the 'Pilgrim Fathers' with prominent internal expansionists and heroes of Indian Wars. These were used in a similar way to the British establishment's practice of using its coloniser heroes of Australia, India and Africa: to promote national and racial myths on the one hand, and justify violent land seizure policies on the other.

In 1873 Plymouth UK had joined in the promotion of the 1620 commemoration with a window in the Guildhall depicting the Mayflower. With the advent of steam ships, Plymouth and Southampton were able in a small way to attract the Pilgrim descendants, eager to see their roots and those of the USA. By the 300-year tercentenary anniversary in 1920 the English too were keen to join in the commemoration business. The election in Plymouth UK in 1919 of the first woman MP in the UK to take her seat in the House of Commons, Nancy Astor, was used to promote the UK's week long 300-year commemoration, as Astor had been born in the USA. Prime Minister David Lloyd George also sent greetings, highlighting that the Pilgrim spirit was '*just as much needed now*' in order to '*revive in the minds of the modern world the ideals of which the Puritan Fathers stood so steadfastly.*'[86]

The 350th Anniversary becomes *The Day of Mourning*

> *We didn't land on Plymouth Rock; the rock was landed on us. We were brought here against our will; we were not brought here to be made citizens.*
> Malcolm X, 29th March 1964

By the 1960s new Black opposition movements to racism were growing in both Britain and the USA. In the Americas, Indigenous Nations, like the African-Americans, were also building on earlier campaigns by re-launching their own distinct movements to both undo colonial expansion and fight for civil and land rights. For example, in the USA the *Indians of All Tribes* reclamation of Alcatraz Island 1969-1971, and the work of such organizations as the *National Indian Youth Council* (NIYC) and the *American Indian Movement* (AIM). It was against this background that the 350 anniversary commemorations of the Mayflower sailing were organised in 1970.

---

86 Angela Bartie, Linda Fleming, Mark Freeman, Tom Hulme, Alex Hutton, Paul Readman, '*Historical Mayflower Pageant', The Redress of the Past,*
http://www.historicalpageants.ac.uk/pageants/1166/

In Plymouth UK the 350th year commemorations included new tourist hotels, celebratory parades and events, and the publication of historical books.[87] However, the Massachusetts commemorations became an occasion for challenge to the sanitisation of the Mayflower Story.

Three hundred fifty years after the Pilgrims began their invasion of the land of the Wampanoag, their "American" descendants planned an anniversary celebration. Still clinging to the white schoolbook myth of friendly relations between their forefathers and the Wampanoag, the anniversary planners thought it would be nice to have an Indian make an appreciative and complimentary speech at their state dinner. Frank James was asked to speak at the celebration. He accepted. The planners, however, asked to see his speech in advance of the occasion, and it turned out that Frank James' views - based on history rather than mythology - were not what the Pilgrims' descendants wanted to hear. Frank James refused to deliver a speech written by a public relations person. Frank James did not speak at the anniversary celebration, Instead the speech was delivered on Thanksgiving Day 1970 on Cole Hill, Plymouth Massachusetts. Since 1970, every Thanksgiving Day on Cole Hill the United American Indians of New England (UAINE) have organized a day of mourning.[88]

87 Gill, C, 1970, *Mayflower Remembered: A history of the Plymouth Pilgrims*, Newton Abbot: David & Charles.
88 http://www.uaine.org/suppressed_speech.htm

Politics and Commemorations

What is commemorated by a nation, a people, or a movement changes according to which section of a society is organising the remembrance. Also commemorations change with the society over time, and can both reinforce and reflect conflicts over the meaning of historical events. Commemorations that relate to European colonialism have illustrated this sharply.

The Curse of Columbus

Take the Columbus quincentenary events of 1992. The official worldwide commemorations adopted the view that Columbus initiated an "Encounter of Two Worlds". It is estimated that some 30 countries established a commemorative organisation of some kind to prepare for 1992, with individual regions and cities in some countries setting up local commemorative bodies too. In addition, UNESCO and other international organisations join them in promoting a "Programme for the Celebration of the Five Hundredth Anniversary of the Encounter of Two Worlds" drawn up in 1988. International stunts included Regatta de Cadiz, a boat race following Columbus's route, and the wedding on Valentine's Day 1992 of Barcelona's Columbus statue and the Statue of Liberty. The tone of the commemoration was not only celebratory of Columbus' original invasion, but was also nostalgic for the colonial period that followed it and its legacies in the Americas.

Some Indigenous Nations have made representations to international bodies in their fight for justice. In 1923, Deskaheh, Chief of the *Iroquois Longhouse* (Haudenosaunee) attempted to speak at the League of Nations in Switzerland but was denied a hearing. More recently attempts to gain an international voice have proved more successful. These have included UN related conferences, for examples those held in 1971, 1977, 1978, 1981, culminating in the Human Rights Council adoption of the *United Nations Declaration on the Rights of Indigenous Peoples* in 2006, ratified by the General Assembly September 2007.

Other international institutional actions have included: *The International Non-Governmental Organization Conference on Discrimination Against Indigenous Populations in the Americas* (organized as a project of the *NGO Sub-Committee on Racism, Racial Discrimination, Apartheid and Colonialism*); The 1986 Quito international declaration by the indigenous peoples of Latin America; the successful campaign for the ILO to adopt the *Convention on*

Indigenous and Tribal Peoples (no. 169, 1989). Indigenous peoples also have invoked procedures within the *Organization of American States*, particularly its *Inter-American Commission on Human Rights*.

Drawing upon their experience of fighting for their rights through international bodies, the Indigenous Nations in the Americas included such tactics in their opposition to the preparations of the Columbus 500-year anniversary celebrations. In 1982 there was a walkout in the UN by African Nations at a proposal by Spain and the Vatican to celebrate Columbus's "encounter" in 1492. In the summer of 1990, 350 representatives from American indigenous groups from all over the hemisphere, met in Quito, Ecuador, at the first *Intercontinental Gathering of Indigenous People in the Americas,* to mobilize against the quincentennial celebration of Columbus Day. The following summer, in Davis, California, more than a hundred Native Americans gathered for a follow-up meeting to the Quito conference. They declared October 12, 1992, "*International Day of Solidarity with Indigenous People*".

Jamestown 2007
These actions alone should have alerted future commemorators to the likelihood of protests if they attempted something similar. However, preparations for the 400-anniversary of the establishment of the Virginia Colony in 1607 were initially in 2000 entitled the commemoration "celebrations". They also referred to colonial invasion and enslavement as "cultural encounters". Some, like Mike Litterst, spokesman for the *Colonial National Historic Park* tried to make concessions and advocated the commemoration "*tell the story of Jamestown as the place where the people of three cultures came together*". But such linguistic disguising of genocide, land grabbing and slavery didn't satisfy the indigenous peoples of the region and the local African American communities who sought to have the oppression of colonialism featured much more to the fore. As a result, not only was any formal labelling of the commemoration as celebration dropped, but the organisers were pushed to concede events organised by Indigenous Nations under the heading *Virginia Indians: 400 Years of Survival*, and African American events through the *Virginia African American Forum* (VAAF).

Unfortunately, in the education sphere, despite conceding that Jamestown's education materials had to include worksheets on slavery, Powhatan Living, etc., such historically corrective materials were the exception. The education aspects of the commemorations were couched in the following terms: "*Jamestown established the culture that would flourish and leave the legacies of free enterprise, rule of law, representative government and cultural diversity. With the assistance of several state and national partners, educational programs and events are focusing attention on these legacies*". The self-congratulatory tone adopted by *Jamestown 2007* determined the terms in which "The Legacies of Jamestown" were to be studied. The commemoration organisers promoted "*Jamestown and the new nation to which it would give rise*", as … "*not the product of a single source or event, but rather evolved out of a rich confluence of ideas and experiences. Contributions made first by Native American, European, and African cultures fostered what is today one of the most pluralistic and diverse societies on earth*".

Alternative

However, there is an alternative. Since 2010, the city of Hampton and several organizations, including *Project 1619,* have observed an annual *African Landing Commemoration Day* on August 20th. The date has been chosen as it is the anniversary of the first documented arrival of Africans in British North America and the establishment of the British Trans-Atlantic slave trade, as well as slavery itself in the British colonies, and, subsequently, in the United States. Hampton History Museum curator Allen Hoilman said,

> *The Angolans that were brought here came from a vibrant, sophisticated civilization. If they survived that terrible voyage, they would have been brought to this culture that is barely surviving and hanging on.*

The *Zinn Education Project - Teaching A People's History* and *Rethinking Schools* have, over the last few years produced a wealth of materials for teachers wishing to correct the bias on Columbus and Discovery.[89] *The People vs. Columbus, et al.* is a role play for students that begins with the premise that a monstrous crime was committed in the years after 1492, when perhaps as many as three million or more Taínos on the island of Hispaniola lost their lives.

In preparation for class, the names of all the "defendants" are listed on the board: Columbus, Columbus' men, King Ferdinand and Queen Isabella, the Taínos, and the System of Empire. Then, in groups, students will portray the

---

89 https://zinnedproject.org/
https://www.rethinkingschools.org/

defendants and the teacher is the prosecutor. The students' responsibility will be: a) to defend themselves against the charges, and b) to explain who they think is guilty and why. This role play is from *Rethinking Columbus: The Next 500 Years*, which includes more context for the events dealt with in the trial, including *The Taínos: Men of the Good*, by José Barriero; a critical reading activity of Columbus's diary on his first contact with Indigenous people; and an adaptation from the writings of Bartolomé de las Casas on the first Spanish priest to denounce the Spanish brutality in Hispaniola.[90]

200th Anniversary of the Abolition of the Slave Trade 2007

The standard British historiography of the abolition of slavery celebrates the abolition of the slave-trade in 1807 as an act of unselfish Christian charity, best summed up by the inscription on the tombstone, in Westminster Abbey, of William Wilberforce, the man who, we are repeatedly told, "freed the slaves".

HIS NAME WILL EVER BE SPECIALLY IDENTIFIED WITH THOSE EXERTIONS WHICH, BY THE BLESSING OF GOD, REMOVED FROM ENGLAND THE GUILT OF THE AFRICAN SLAVE TRADE

Suddenly, the British are turned into the heroes rather than the villains of the story. Little is said about the massive compensation paid to the slave-owners when slavery itself was finally abolished.[91]

By this stroke of genius, radicalism was undermined and the compensation was largely paid by the workers as, in those days, the majority of state revenue was raised by regressive taxation on items of basic consumption, which always hits the poor hardest. Also, both the ongoing involvement of British companies who continued unofficially in the slave trade after 1807 and British investment in slave production outside the Empire after the abolition of slavery, are rarely mentioned.[92] The British establishment has boasted ever since the passing of abolition laws of its freedom-loving generosity.

---

90 Bigelow, Bill & Bob Peterson (Editors), 1998, *Rethinking Columbus: The Next 500 Years*, Milwaukee: Rethinking Schools.
91 Hall, Catherine; Nicholas Draper; Keith McClelland; Katie Donington and Rachel Lang, 2014, *Legacies of British Slave-Ownership, Colonial Slavery and the Formation of Victorian Britain*, Cambridge: Cambridge University Press.
92 Sherwood, Marika, 2007, *After Abolition: Britain and the Slave Trade since 1807*, London, I.B. Tauris.

Slave Rebellions

Even less is said about the slave rebellions or the radical reformers in Britain who linked abolition of slavery to egalitarian reforms in Britain. We are rarely told that Olaudah Equiano, the famous author of a book describing his life while enslaved, was a leading member of the radical *London Corresponding Society*. In his book he clearly linked the slave-owners to the corrupt political establishment that they were fighting in Britain. Equiano argued that the end of slavery would reduce the reactionary political base of Old Corruption, as many West Indian planters controlled the so-called Rotten Boroughs, where the Member of Parliament was effectively appointed by a rich man who controlled the electors. Any attempt at reform of the undemocratic electoral system in Britain would bring the reformers into head-on collision with the entrenched landed elite and their allies among the slave-holders.[93] Thus, the struggle for reform in Britain and the campaign for the abolition of slavery became linked as part of the radical popular democratic movement of the late 18th century, with its demands for political and human rights.

But it would be a mistake to see emancipation as simply arising from British politics, whether radical, moderate or conservative. The enslaved themselves played an essential part in their own liberation. The revolution in Haiti in 1791, not only freed the slaves on what was probably the most important sugar colony of the time, it also made the slave-owners on other islands realise the precarious nature of their position and required an increasing militarisation of the region. The Baptist War, as the 1831 Jamaica uprising became known, can be credited with concentrating the minds of the British Government to face the fact that increasing rebelliousness was causing the whole system to fail. Slave revolts, escapes, the formation of Maroon settlements and similar acts of resistance undermined the attractiveness of slavery as an investment proposition, while also heartening radical abolitionist opinion back in Britain.[94]

The 200th anniversary commemoration of the abolition of the slave trade in the UK was marked with coordinated exhibitions and publications in the former principal UK slaving ports of Liverpool, Bristol and Greenwich in London, together with smaller commemoration events in Hull, Plymouth, etc. Black

---

93 Walvin, James, 1977, "The Impact of Slavery on British Radical Politics: 1787-1838, *Annals of the New York Academy of Sciences*, no.292, pp.344-350.
94 Matthews, Gelien, 2006, *Caribbean Slave Revolts and the British Abolitionist Movement*, Baton Rouge: Louisiana State University Press.

community and Black history activists were initially involved in the design of materials in London. However, commemoration organisers were subsequently criticized by some groups and individuals who were used as consultants, for the peremptory way the process of consultation ended. However, Black historians and others involved were widely acknowledged as having ensured that a Black peoples' perspective on slavery was included in the commemorations principally because of their contributions.

Let us leave the last word to Toyin Agbetu who intervened at the 2007 commemorative service held in Westminster Abbey marking the 200th anniversary of the act to abolish the slave trade:

I was moved to make a collective voice heard at the commemorative ritual of appeasement and self-approval marking the bicentenary of the British parliamentary act to abolish what they disingenuously refer to as a "slave trade".

The "Wilberfest" abolition commemoration has eradicated any mention of resistance, rebellion and revolution instigated by millions of African people.

US Soldiers Who Refused to Kill Native Americans at Sand Creek

Every Thanksgiving weekend, Arapaho and Cheyenne youth lead a 180-mile relay from the Sand Creek Massacre National Historic Site to Denver. A sunrise ceremony honours the 200 Arapaho and Cheyenne people who were murdered in the notorious Sand Creek Massacre, carried out by the US Army on the orders of Colonel John Chivington on November 29, 1864. Also honoured are Captain Silas Soule and Lieutenant Joseph Cramer who personally refused to take part in the murder of peaceful people, while ordering the men under their command to stand down. Captain Soule wrote "*that any man who would take part in the murders, knowing the circumstances as we did, was a low lived cowardly son of a bitch. I refused to fire and swore that none but a coward would*".

Cheyenne and Arapaho gather for a sunrise ceremony at Soule's flower-adorned grave at Denver's Riverside Cemetery. The participants then continue into Denver, where a plaque is mounted on the side of an office building at the place where Soule was murdered on April 23, 1865. His death, for which no one was ever brought to justice, occurred only two months after he testified against Chivington before the Army commission. Over the last few decades, Soule's grave and place of death have been transformed into sites of remembrance.[95]

Sand Creek Massacre by Cheyenne eyewitness and artist Howling Wolf - 1875

---

95 Stratton, Billy J, 2017, "Remembering the US soldiers who refused orders to murder Native Americans at Sand Creek", *The Conversation*, November 22.

The Mayflower 400 Education Project

Mayflower 400 did not include Education as an aspect of the commemorations until 2015. However, an educational element had been implicit even when official documents focused almost exclusively on tourism. Education was made explicit in the design and narrative of the revamped Mayflower Museum, and the early posting on the Mayflower 400 website of a large number of education worksheets written by the community investment company, The Real Ideas Organisation (RIO). It was now clear that a similar sanitized version of the Mayflower Story that Plymouth UK had promoted for the 350th year Anniversary in 1970 was being planned for 2020.

What was most striking about both the worksheets and the museum panels was what they left out.

The Mayflower Museum

The Mayflower Museum is positioned opposite the Mayflower Steps in Sutton Harbour, above the Plymouth tourist information centre. In September 2015 a revamped version was opened as part of the preparations for the 2020 Mayflower 400 Commemorations. It advertised its presentation of the Mayflower Story as follows:

> *The Pilgrim Fathers set sail from Plymouth on the Mayflower on 6 September 1620, eventually landing and settling in present-day Plymouth, Massachusetts. The Mayflower Museum explores the story of the Mayflower and the Pilgrim Fathers with information and hands-on displays, including dress-up and role play, a model of the Mayflower built by Devonport Dockyard apprentices in 1969 and a list of all the Pilgrims and their hometowns. Visit the museum and enjoy learning more about this important moment in Plymouth's shared history with America.*

What is most striking about the museum's presentation is that it does not include well-known historical background and context, crucial to understanding the importance of the Mayflower colonization expedition. Indeed, the negative impact of colonialism is limited to two statements:

Land grabbing following the Mayflower settlement is intimated very briefly but only in the following terms: "*This land was the territory of the Native American Lenape Nation, who were unaware that their homeland had been granted to another people*".

The consequences of colonization for the Indigenous Americans is only acknowledged in the following: "*Many Native Americans do not celebrate Thanksgiving but rather observe the annual holiday as a National Day of Mourning, acknowledging the sacrifices of their ancestors as a result of colonization*".

The story the panels explore consists of brief details of Plymouth and its trading and shipping heritage, including the Hawkins family, though no mention is made of the slave trade they pioneered; the passengers (their names, their Puritan religion, where they came from, etc.); the stages of the journeys from Holland and England to the North American coast; extracts from key historical texts (the Mayflower Compact, the Diary of William Bradford, second Governor of the Plymouth Colony, the writings of 'Pilgrim' leaders Robert Cushman and Edward Winslow.); the details of the Mayflower and Speedwell ships and their sea journeys in 1620; their early encounters in what became Plymouth Massachusetts with Indigenous Americans, focusing on the local Sachem, Massasoit, and the two local English speaking Indigenous Americans, Squanto and Samoset.

The Mayflower School Worksheets

The education worksheets, like the museum panels, neglected the fact that the Mayflower journey was a colonising one, and omitted slavery, genocide, land grabbing and war. The worksheets included statements such as the following: "*There is much to understand in regards to the relationship between colonists and Native Americans, you can explore this story further in our Mayflower Exploration section*".[96]

"*The Plymouth colony was one of the earliest North American settlements to be founded by the English – it is from here that the exploration of America began*". [97]

The educational worksheets consisted of: Seven Mayflower Factsheets (The Mayflower Voyage – Journey to the New World; Plymouth Steps; The Mayflower; The Speedwell; The Mayflower Compact; Setting up the Plymouth Colony; The Wampanoag and the First Thanksgiving); Four Online resource pages (The Mayflower Story; The Pilgrims; The Voyage of the Mayflower; Arriving in America); Four Mayflower Detective Resource question sheets,

---

96 *The Wampanoag and the First Thanksgiving Factsheet,* Mayflower 400 education website.
97 *Setting up the Plymouth Colony Factsheet,* Mayflower 400 education website

some linked to online resources; Four Mayflower Challenges Resource sheets; Seven Mayflower Art activity sheets; Two Mayflower Story activity sheets; Two Mayflower Tour Guide activity sheets; On line Mayflower story activity guidance and resources; On line Mayflower talk for writing activity guidance and resources; a series of links to other websites about the Mayflower, the Pilgrims and the Plymouth Colony.

The Mayflower 400 Scheme of Work

In the Summer 2017 the worksheets were taken down from the Mayflower 400 website and 'The Mayflower 400 Scheme of Work' for Key Stage 3 was posted. In the introduction to this first draft of the scheme it was claimed in the "Overall aim" that *"The Mayflower 400 project is an international commemoration of the endeavours of the separatists, who left England, looking for a place away from persecution, and eventually became known as the Mayflower Pilgrims. It is a story of discrimination, determination and hope"*. The "Framework" section explained that the *"Mayflower is the catalyst from which young people can discuss the values of tolerance, resolve and democracy; it is the catalyst from which young people can explore the skills of survival, business and communication. Mayflower's importance lies in its ability to address the value of inclusivity, and how we are able to promote an ethos of cohesion, growth and innovative, pluralistic thinking"*.

Like the museum panels, there was nothing in the 54 pages of the first draft scheme about slavery, war and genocide. Not surprisingly, the scheme joined the museum panels as a focus of local criticism and protest over the education aspects of the Mayflower commemorations.

In late January 2018 a second draft of the Key Stage 3 scheme was posted replacing the 2017 one. Not only were the offensive claims of the introduction to the first draft gone, but also a new module, *History and the Native American Wars*, had been added, and this module DID mention slavery, war and genocide. In addition, the introduction now included: *"understand the experiences and rights of the Native Americans; understand the challenging cultural debates around the legacy of colonization; understand the significance of the impact on indigenous populations"*, and several modules now had references to Native Americans inserted into them.

Remembering Colonization

There are many lessons that the history of commemorations has to teach. These include those from the Mayflower commemorations going back to the 18th century; the commemorations of the Columbus 500th year anniversary; the Virginia Colony 400-year anniversary commemoration; the abolition of the slave trade 200-year anniversary commemoration.

The Indigenous Nations of North America, together with African Americans and African Caribbean peoples, are the best placed to determine how the Mayflower journey and settlements should be remembered. But those who organised commemorations in the past have, in the main, ignored these groups, and the tradition of placing the journey of the English Separatists at the centre of the Mayflower Story still needs to be challenged. Ignoring, relegating or minimizing colonialism and slavery presents a sanitized account of history. The involvement of all the relevant communities in planning the education part of such remembrances is crucial. Foremost are those communities who continue to live with, and continue to struggle to overcome, the consequences of colonialism and slavery. In addition, there are groups, local and otherwise, of people involved in education. In Plymouth UK the local schools' education union was among the first to publicly protest at the initial sanitized commemoration plans.

The Mayflower 400th year anniversary commemoration has the potential to start to move away from the established sanitising tradition. This requires acknowledging that the Mayflower journey was part of early English colonialism, with all that implies. But are the changes recently made to one of their education schemes a first step in that direction? Will this change to one document be followed by an overhauling of the planning of actual teaching materials (still to be created at time of writing, 2018), their teacher training plans and the Mayflower Museum panels? While on the one hand Mayflower 400 education organisers post a single new module on their website, on the other they publish a recruitment advert for "*Mayflower 400 school coordinators*" which speaks of "*projects to mark the important CELEBRATION*". Also of concern are the teaching resources that have so far been made available. The newly posted worksheets do not address, or even mention, the themes of slavery and genocide. Neither do they mention events such as the 'Trail of tears', the 1830 Removal Act, the Removal of Confederate Statutes, the continued marginalisation of Native Americans, and Standing

Rock, which are very briefly referred to in their "History and the Native American Wars" module.

'Every child in Plymouth will know the story of the Mayflower'
(Plymouth Council Scrutiny committee, 16/03/2016)

Perhaps.

But in 2018 the question remains: will the organisers of the 400th year Mayflower Anniversary break with the inglorious tradition of sanitising the Mayflower Story?

The Pilgrim Fathers Memorial to Separatist members of Scrooby congregation arrested in 1607, is located on the north bank of The Haven, near Boston, Lincolnshire, UK.

Bibliography

Bailey, Ronald, 1994, "The Other Side of Slavery: Black Labor, Cotton, and Textile Industrialization in Great Britain and the United States." *Agricultural History*, Vol. 68, no. 2, pp. 35–50.

Bailey, Ronald, 1990, "The Slave(ry) Trade and the Development of Capitalism in the United States: The Textile Industry in New England," *Social Science History*, 14, no.3, pp.373-414.

Baptist, Edward, 2015, *The Half Has Never Been Told*, New York: Basic Books.

Bohrer, Ashley, 2018, "Just Wars of Accumulation: the Salamanaca School, Race and Colonial Capitalism", *Race & Class*, Jan 2018, Vol. 56, no.3.

Bunker, N, 2010, *Making Haste From Babylon: The Mayflower Pilgrims and Their World: a new history*, London: Bodley Head.

Borucki, A. et al, 2015, "Atlantic History and the Slave Trade to Spanish America", *American Historical Review* 120, no. 2 (2015): 433–61.

Calder, Angus, 1998, *Revolutionary Empire: The Rise of the English-Speaking Empire from the Fifteenth Century to the 1780s*, London: Pimlico.

Carrington, Selwyn, 1987, "The American Revolution and the British West Indies' Economy" *The Journal of Interdisciplinary History*, 17, no. 4.

Cheetham, J K, 2001, *On The Trail of the Pilgrim Fathers*, Edinburgh: Luath.

Cozzens, Peter, 2016, *The Earth Is Weeping*, London: Atlantic Books.

Dunbar-Ortiz, Roxanne, 2018, "Loaded: a Disarming History of the Second Amendment", *Monthly Review*, Jan 2018.

Dunbar-Ortiz, Roxanne, 2016, *All the Real Indians Died Off and 20 Other Myths About Native Americans, Boston*, USA: Beacon Press.

Dunbar-Ortiz, Roxanne, 2014, *An Indigenous Peoples' History of the United States*, Boston: USA, Beacon Press

Evans, James, 2017, *Emigrants: why the English sailed to the New World*. Orio: W&N.

Farrow, Anne; Lang, Joel and Frank, Jenifer, 2008, *Complicity: How the North Promoted, Prolonged, and Profited from Slavery*, New York: Ballantine.

Foner, Eric and John A. Garraty, 1991, *The Reader's Companion to American History*. Boston: Houghton-Mifflin.

Fuentes, Marisa J. and White, Deborah Gray (eds), 2016, *Scarlet and Black: Slavery and Dispossession in Rutgers History*, New Brunswick: Rutgers University Press.

Gaskill, M, 2014, *Between Two Worlds: How the English Became Americans*, Oxford: Oxford University Press.

Genovese, Eugene, 1984 edn, *In Red and Black: Marxian explorations in Southern and Afro-American History*, Knoxville: University of Tennessee Press.

Gill, C, 1970, *Mayflower Remembered: A history of the Plymouth Pilgrims*, Newton Abbot: David & Charles.

Gragg, Larry D, 1993, "A Puritan in the West Indies: The Career of Samuel Winthrop." *The William and Mary Quarterly* 50, no. 4 pp.768-86.

Grann, David, 2017, *Killers of the Flower Moon: Oil, Money, Murder and the Birth of the FBI*, New York City: Simon and Schuster.

Greene, Lorenzo, 1928, "Slave-Holding New England and Its Awakening." *The Journal of Negro History* 13, no. 4 pp.492-533.

Greene, Lorenzo, 1942, *The Negro in Colonial New England, 1620-1776*. New York: Columbia University Press.

Grenier, John, 2008, *The First Way of War: American War Making on the Frontier 1607 - 1814*, Cambridge: Cambridge University Press.

Heath, D B, 1963, *Mourt's Relation: a Journal of the Plymouth Pilgrims*, Massachusetts: Applewood Books.

Horne, Gerald, 2018, *The Apocalypse of Settler Colonialism: The Roots of Slavery, White Supremacy, and Capitalism in Seventeenth-Century North America and the Caribbean*, New York: Monthly Review.

Jennings, F, 1976, *The Invasion of America: Indians, Colonialism and the Cant of Conquest*, New York, Norton & Co.

Jordan, Winthrop, 1961, "The Influence of the West Indies on the Origins of New England Slavery." *The William and Mary Quarterly* 18, no. 2 pp.243-50.

Klein, Herbert, 1978, *The Middle Passage: Comparative Studies in the Atlantic Slave Trade*, Princeton: Princeton University Press.

Lepore, Jill, 1999, *The Name of War: King Philip's War and the Origins of American Identity*, New York, Vintage Books.

Madley, Benjamin, 2016, *An American Genocide, The United States and the California Catastrophe*, 1846-1873, London, Yale University Press.

Mather, Cotton, 1706, *The Negro Christianized: An Essay to Excite and Assist that Good Work, the Instruction of Negro-Servants in Christianity*, Boston: Green.

Morgan, Edmund, 1964, *The Founding of Massachusetts: Historians and the Sources*, Indianapolis: Bobbs-Merrill.

Newell, Margaret Ellen, 2015, *Brethren by Nature: New England Colonists and the Origin of American Slavery*, New York: Cornell University Press..

Newell, Margaret Ellen, 2003, '*Economy*', in Vickes, Daniel (Ed.), *A Companion to Colonial America*, Oxford: Blackwell.

Ogden, Nancy, Catherine Perkins, and David M. Donahue, 2008, "Not a Peculiar Institution: Challenging Students' Assumptions about Slavery in U.S. History." *The History Teacher* 41, no. 4: 469-88.

Parker, Matthew, 2011, *The Sugar Barons: Family, Corruption, Empire and War*, London: Hutchinson.

Philbrick, N, 2007, *Mayflower: A Voyage to War* London: Harper Perennial.

Phillips, Ulrich, 1918, *American Negro Slavery: A Survey of the Supply, Employment and Control of Negro Labor as Determined by the Plantation Régime*, New York: Appleton.

Pilgrim Society, 1871, *The Proceedings at the celebration by the Pilgrim Society at Plymouth, December 21, 1870 of the two hundred and fiftieth anniversary of the landing of the pilgrims*, Plymouth: John Wilson and Son.

Quigley, L, 2012, *Blood British History: Plymouth*, Stroud: The History Press.

Race & Class (1992) "The Curse of Columbus", Jan 1992, Vol. 33, no.3

Richter, Daniel (2001) *Facing East from Indian Country: A Native History of Early America* Cambridge, Mass: Harvard UP.

Resendez, Andres, 2016, *The Other Slavery*, Boston, Houghton.

Sherwood, Marika, 2007, *After Abolition: Britain and the Slave Trade since 1807*, London, I.B. Tauris.

Shorto, Russell, 2014, *The Island at the Centre of the World*, London: Abacus.

Thomas, G E, 1975, "Puritans, Indians, and the Concept of Race", *The New England Quarterly* 48, no. 1 pp.3-27.

Thomas, Hugh (1997) *The Slave Trade: the History of the Atlantic Slave Trade 1440-1870*, London, Picador.

United Nations, 2010, '*Impact on Indigenous Peoples of the International Legal construct known as the Doctrine of Discovery, which has served as the Foundation of the Violation of their Human Rights*', Tonya Gonnella Frichner author of E/C.19/2010/13, New York, UN Economic and Social Council.

Von Frank, Albert J, 1994, "John Saffin: Slavery and Racism in Colonial Massachusetts." *Early American Literature* 29, no. 3, pp.254-72.

Warren, Wendy, 2016, *New England Bound: Slavery and Colonization in early America*, New York: W.W. Norton & Co.

Winthrop, John, 1908, *Winthrop's journal: "History of New England", 1630-1649*, New York: Scribner.

Young, Alexander, 1841, *Chronicles of the Pilgrim Fathers of the Colony of Plymouth, from 1602-1625*, Boston: Little and Brown.

Mayflower - a brief selective timeline to aid contextualisation of events.[98]

1450 - 1600

1452 & 1455 *Doctrine of Discovery* Papal Bulls issued, permitting Portugal to seize land and slaves in West Africa.

1482 Columbus visit to the Portuguese trading & slaving base, Sao Jorge da Mina, on the African Guinea coast.

1492 Columbus's first voyage across the Atlantic to "La Isla Espanola" in the Caribbean. 12 indigenous people captured to be used as show-pieces in Spain.

---

98 This brief timeline has been created to aid the reader in reconsidering 'The Mayflower Story' that has traditionally been told without historical contextualisation. It is not offered as a substitute for a historical timeline of slavery and genocide in the Americas. Similarly, while it is hoped that the bibliography of references in this pamphlet will aid further study and reflection on the Mayflower 400-anniversary commemorations, it is not offered as a substitute for a bibliography on slavery and genocide in the Americas.

1493 Papal Bull *Inter Cetera* granting to Spain the right to conquer the lands which Columbus had already found, as well as any lands which Spain might "discover" in the future.

1494 Treaty of Tordesillas divided lands outside Europe between the Portuguese Empire and the Crown of Castile.

1495 During Columbus' second journey to the Caribbean, the practice of capturing Indigenous people in the Americas for use as slaves starts.

1496 King Henry VII gave an English Crown licence to John Cabot's voyage to Newfoundland.

1502 A fleet of 30 Spanish ships brought the new Governor Nicolas de Ovando, hundreds of Spanish settlers, and an estimated 100 enslaved Africans to Hispaniola.

1502 Estimated population of *La Isla Espanola* as 200,000 – 300,000.

1508 Estimated population of *La Isla Espanola* as 60,000.

1512 Prominent Indigenous leader in Espanola and Cuba, Hatuey, a Taino cacique [leader], executed. His armed resistance campaign started during the Columbus period.

1513 'Indian' slavery systematised in Spanish colonies in the Americas under the 'encomienda' system.

1514 Census of population of *La Isla Espanola* as 26,000.

1517 Estimated of the population of *La Isla Espanola* 11,000.

1518 First reports of smallpox cases in the Caribbean. No evidence of smallpox prior to 1518.

1542 The "New Laws" abolish Indian slavery in Spanish colonies in the Americas. However, in order to supply workers in the new silver mines a system of nominal wages for compulsory labour, known as *Repartimiento de Indios*, is introduced.

1562 and 1564 first two 'successful' slaving ventures by Sir John Hawkins.

1567 'Unsuccessful' slaving venture by Sir John Hawkins, demonstrates the need for English colonial bases.

1584 and 1587 attempts to found the English Colony of Roanoke in modern day North Carolina.

1600 - 1700

1606 Establishment of the Plymouth Company (The Virginia Company of Plymouth). Territorial allocation between the coastal strip of 38th and 45th parallels. Subsequently used by the Crown to claim the area that included early New England.

1606 Establishment of the Virginia Company (The Virginia Company of London).

1607 Establishment of the first continuous English Colony, the Virginia Colony in Jamestown by The Virginia Company of London. The Colonists adopted Feedfight tactics against the *Powhatans*.

1607 failed attempt to found an English Colony in Maine by the Plymouth Company.

1607 imprisonment of some Separatist Puritans from Scrooby, Yorkshire. Start of move by Separatists to Leiden in Holland.

1610 Virginian Governor Gates ordered an attack on the *Paspahegh's* villages to eradicate them.

1614 The Dutch New Netherlands Company establish a trading post on Manhattan Island near the Hudson River.

1619 Plans by the Leiden-based English Separatists to move to America formulated: 1st use patent obtained from the Virginia company to go to Virginia Colony; 2nd Dutch offer to help establish a settlement on or near Dutch claimed colonial settlement region; 3rd Patent obtained by Merchant adventurers from the Virginia company to go to the north part of the Virginia Colony near the mouth of the Hudson River. 3rd plan accepted.

1619 First African Slaves imported into the Virginia Colony.

1619 First colonial assembly started in the Virginia Colony.

1620 Mayflower voyage.

1619 - 22   3,000 of the 3600 settlers who arrived in the Virginia Colony died .

1622 *Powhatan* Confederacy under Opechancanough attack on Jamestown killing 350 colonists.

1622 Mayflower passenger accounts of their journey published as "Mourt's Relations".

1623 *Wessagusset*, near New Plymouth Colony the scene of the killing of six members of the Massachusetts Indigenous Nation by Myles Standish's armed group.

1624 Edward Winslow's, "Good News from New England", published.

1626 The Dutch West India Company imports 11 male slaves of African heritage into the New Netherlands Colony, which later shared borders with early New England colonies.

1636 Colonial North America's slave trade begins when the first American slave carrier, Desire, is built and launched in Massachusetts.

1636 - 38 *Pequot* War.

1638 Start of importation of slaves of African heritage from the Caribbean into New England and export of Pequot slaves to the Caribbean.

1641 Massachusetts Bay is the first English colony to legalize slavery.

1643 Estimated colonial settler population of New England 20,000.

1644 - 46 Tideswater War, Virginia: two years of raids on Indigenous peoples' villages and fields using starvation to clear the James Valley.

1623 - 55 English Caribbean Colonies founded - St. Kitts (1623), Barbados (1627), Nevis (1628), Providence (1630), Antigua (1632), Monserrat (1632), Anguilla (1650) and Jamaica (1655). 1640s an estimated 19,000 African Slaves imported into Barbados.

1665 - 67 Anglo-Dutch War. England won, resulting in the New Netherlands Colony being declared English colonial territory (parts of modern day New York, New Jersey, Connecticut, Pennsylvania, and Delaware) and New Amsterdam becoming New York.

1672 the slave trade systematized through the Royal African Company under the English Crown.

1675 - 76 'King Philip's War'.

1643 84 United Colonies of New England (UCNE) alliance.

1689 - 98 'The Nine-Years' War' between European powers was known in the Americas as 'King William's War'.

1600 - 1700 90% Drop in the Indigenous population of the colonised territories of New England.

1641 - 1700 15,000 Africans were brought to North America and 308,000 to the English Caribbean.[99]

1700 - 1776

1712 Slaves in New York City revolt. 19 slave executions follow.

1702 - 13 'The War of the Spanish Succession' between England and an alliance of France and Spain, was known in the Americas as 'Queen Anne's War'. It was fought in three areas Florida/ Carolina, New England and what is now south eastern Canada. Like other Inter-European wars of the 18th century, it involved several Indigenous Nations and massacres, e.g. the Apalachee massacre of 1704. The Peace of Utrecht, which ended the war, effectively gave Britain an increased share of the European slave trade.

1744 - 48 The War of the Austrian Succession between European powers was known in the Americas as King George's War.

1754 - 63 The French and Indian War ends with firstly, The Treaty of Paris (France ceded its claimed colonial territories including parts of what is now Canada and the Ohio and Mississippi valleys), and, secondly, George III's Royal Proclamation which creates a western boundary for English colonisation in North America.

1763 - 66 Pontiac's War.

1769 Forefathers Day started in Plymouth Massachusetts.

1775 - 1900

1775 - 83 'American War of Independence'/ 'American Revolution' involving Indigenous Nations. British defeat in the war included its First Nation allies, notably the Iroquois Confederacy, who, together with loyalist colonists, were dispossessed. Many moved to 'Upper Canada' and some First Nations allied to the British were, 'allocated' land there.

1787 Northwest Ordinance - a colonization procedure involving military occupation of Indigenous Nation.

1790 - 95 The Ohio Indian War.

---

99 Borucki, A. et al, 2015, "Atlantic History and the Slave Trade to Spanish America", *American Historical Review* 120, no. 2, p.440.

1500 - 1800 In the 16th century, more than five million Native people lived in the conterminous United States area. By the nineteenth century, that number had been reduced 90% to 600,000.

1791 - 1804 Haitian Revolution ends slavery in the former French colony of Saint-Domingue, the western part of 'La Isla Espanola'.

1803 the Louisiana Purchase - 828,000 square miles (2,144,520 square km) claimed by France sold to the US Government, which doubled the size of the United States.

1807 British Slave Trade Act outlawed slave trading in the British Empire, but slave smuggling continues.

1808 United States bans the importing of slaves of African heritage, but smuggling continues.

1810 - 13 The Northwest Indian War.

1813 - 14 The Creek War.

1812 - 15 War between Britain & Canada and the USA that involved Indigenous Nations.

1817 - 19 First Seminole War.

1700 - 1820 Drop in population of West Africa in the slave taking zone estimated at 5 million (i.e. 20% of 1700 figure).

1820 Missouri Compromise - Missouri is admitted to the Union as a slave state, Maine as a free state. Slavery is forbidden in any subsequent territories north of latitude 360 30'.

1822 South Carolina Freed slave Denmark Vesey attempts a rebellion in Charleston. 35 participants are hanged.

1823 US Supreme Court ruling in the case of Johnson & Graham's Lessee v. M'Intosh used the Doctrine of Discovery to reach its decision.

1830 Removal Act.

1831 Virginia Slave preacher Nat Turner leads a two-day uprising against whites, killing about 60 people. Nat Turner was eventually caught and hanged.

1831 In the case of the Cherokee Nation v Georgia, the US Supreme Court ruled that Indigenous Nations were 'domestic dependent nations'.

1831 Slave revolt in Jamaica (20,000 slaves took part) greatly hastened the abolition of British slavery.

1833 Slavery Abolition Act outlawed slavery in the British Empire.

1835 - 42 Second Seminole War.

1847 Residential boarding schools for First Nation children in Canada started. Ended 1996.

1846 - 48 Mexican-American War. Defeated Mexico yields an enormous amount of territory to the United States.

1855 - 58 Third Seminole War.

1856 William Bradford's 'Of Plymouth Plantation' published.

1860 Bureau of Indian Affairs starts residential boarding schools for children of Indigenous Nations in USA.

1862 Homestead Act - 300,000,000 acres appropriated from Indigenous Nations.

1862 Pacific Railroad Act - nearly 200,000,000 acres appropriated from Indigenous Nations and transferred to private companies.

1862 Dakota War.

1863 Emancipation Proclamation that all slaves in Rebel territory are free.

1864 Sand Creek massacre.

1861 - 65 United States Civil War

1865 13th Amendment to the USA constitution outlawing slavery and 'involuntary servitude' passed.

1867 Peonage Abolition Act passed directed at this specific form of involuntary servitude practiced against Indigenous Americans, particularly in the New Mexico territory.

1871 Indian Appropriation Act enabled the US Government to make laws affecting Indigenous Nations with or without their consent.

1871 102,000 census estimate of the size of the 'Aboriginal population' in Canada Population estimates for the end of 15th century 500,000 – 2 million.

1846 - 1873 9,400 to 16,000 California 'Indians' were killed by 'non-Indians', most in 370 massacres. Estimated population decline of these 'Californian' Nations overall in this period - 100,000.

1873 Cypress Hills massacre, Saskatchewan, Canada

1876 Indian Act in Canada severely restricted First Nation peoples' rights and introduced assimilation regulations.

1879 'Carlisle Indian Boarding Schools' begin in USA.

1887 General Allotment Act. As a result of this law and 1898 Curtis Act - the loss of territory of the Indigenous Nations greatly increased. Land designated as Indian decreased from 156 million acres in 1881 to 50 million acres in 1934

1890 Wounded Knee massacre.

YEAR	USA LAND AREA (Sq Miles)	Indigenous population 1800-90
1800	334562	600,000
1810	396990	535,000
1820	502104	471,000
1830	615041	440,000
1840	801294	400,000
1850	946098	365,000
1860	1132024	308,000
1870	1243150	278,000
1880	1488872	244,000
1890	1812484	228,000

1492 - 1900 it is estimated that in this period in the Americas there were in total, 2.5 to 5 million indigenous slaves, of which 147,000 – 340,000 were enslaved in North America.

1900 - 2018

1871 - 1921 The British Crown 'entered into' 11 'numbered treaties' with several First Nations in Canada, which resulted in large losses of land of these Nations in Northern Ontario, Manitoba, Saskatchewan, Alberta, and parts of the Yukon, the Northwest Territories and British Columbia. The treaties were for the spread of European settlements, the railway system and resource extraction.

1924 Indian Citizenship Act granted citizenship to about 125,000 of 300,000 indigenous people in the United States.

1934 Indian Reorganisation Act.

1937 Columbus Day gained federal status in the USA.

1948 Native Americans who were granted citizenship rights under the 1924 Act but denied it under state laws, gain citizenship.

1970 The practice of having a day of mourning on Thanksgiving Day on Cole Hill, Plymouth Massachusetts started. United American Indians of New England (UAINE) continue to organise a day of mourning every Thanksgiving Day on Cole Hill.

1982 a walkout in the UN by African Nations at a Spanish and Vatican proposal to celebrate Columbus's 'encounter' in 1492.

1992 Columbus quincentenary.

2000 the head of the United States Bureau of Indian Affairs (BIA) formally apologized for the agency's participation in the "ethnic cleansing" of Western tribes.

2007 400-year anniversary commemoration of the establishment of the Virginia Colony titled Jamestown 2007.

2007 200-year anniversary commemoration of the abolition by Britain of the slave trade.

2007 UN Declaration on the Rights of Indigenous Peoples (UNDRIP) Four counties vote against its adoption – Australia, Canada, New Zealand, USA. Australia agreed to the declaration in 2009, New Zealand in 2010, USA 2011, Canada in 2016.

ZINN EDUCATION PROJECT

ABOLISH COLUMBUS DAY

SOLIDARITY WITH INDIGENOUS PEOPLES

RESOURCES · INFORMATION · CONNECT
www.zinnedproject.org/ABOLISH

The Socialist History Society

The Socialist History Society was founded in 1992 and includes many leading Socialist and labour historians, academic and amateur researchers, in Britain and overseas. The SHS holds regular events, public meeting controversies. We produce a range of publications, including the journal Socialist History and a regular Newsletter.

The SHS is the successor to the Communist Party History Group, which was established in 1946 and is now totally independent of all political parties and groups. We are engaged in and seek to encourage historical studies from a Marxist and broadly-defined left perspective. We are interested in all aspects of human history from the earliest social formations to the present day and aim for an international approach.

We are particularly interested in the various struggles of labour, of women, of progressive campaigns and peace movements around the world, as well as the history of colonial peoples, black people, and all oppressed communities seeking justice, human dignity and liberation.

Each year we produce two issues of our journal Socialist History, one or two historical pamphlets in our Occasional Publications series, and frequent members' Newsletters. We hold public lectures and seminars mainly in London. In addition, we hold special conferences, book launches and joint events with other friendly groups.

Join the Socialist History Society today!

Members receive all our serial publications for the year at no extra cost and regular mailings about our activities. Members can vote at our AGM and seek election to positions on the committee, and are encouraged to participate in other society activities.

Annual membership fees for 2019 (renewable every January):
Full UK £30.00
Concessionary UK £25.00
Europe full £35.00
Europe concessionary £30.00
Rest of world full £40.00
Rest of world concessionary £35.00

For details of institutional subscriptions, please e-mail the treasurer on francis@socialisthistorysociety.co.uk.

To join the society for 2019, please send your name and address plus a cheque/PO payable to Socialist History Society to: SHS, 50 Elmfield Road, Balham, London SW17 SAL.
You can also pay online.
Visit our websites on www.socialisthistorysociety.co.uk
and www.lwbooks.co.uk/socialist-history

Also see Mayflower Mavericks: https://mayflowermavericks.wordpress.com   @MayflowerM1620